A Guide to Islām's
Inquisitive N
*Neglect...*

THE MEANING OF

# ISLAM

## A Brief Explanation of the Most Important Principles and Teachings

إِنَّ الدِّينَ عِندَ اللَّهِ الإِسْلَامُ

**"Verily, the way (of life) in the sight of Allāh is Islām."** (3:19)


Abu ʿIyāḍ
Amjad bin Muḥammad Rafīq
**www.newmuslim.ws**

Title: The Meaning of Islām
Author: Abū ʿIyāḍ Amjad bin Muḥammad Rafīq

1st edition (3.5) – Jumādā al-Thānī 1438 / March 2017

http://www.newmuslim.ws

ISBN 13: 978-1-64007-380-7
ISBN 10: 1-64007-380-9



For further information contact:

**Wright Street Masjid**
472 Coventry Road
Small Heath
Birmingham B10 0UG
United Kingdom
t. +44 (0) 121 773 0033
e. admin@spubs.com

**Masjid Bin Baz**
East Road (next to no. 2)
Plaistow
London E15 3QR
United Kingdom
e. info@al-athariyyah.com

**Masjid al-Sunnah**
3 Paternoster Lane
Bradford BD7 3DS
United Kingdom
t. +44 (0) 1274 501 736
e. info@albaseerah.com

**Germantown Masjid**
4944 Germantown Avenue
Philadelphia
PA 19144
United States
t. +1 215 848 2615
e. admin@germantownmasjid.com

**Masjid al-Furqan**
874-A Weston Road
Toronto
Ontario M6N 3R6
Canada
t. +1 416 243 5320
e. info@troid.ca

# Contents

# Transliteration Table

## Consonants

| | | | | | | | |
|---|---|---|---|---|---|---|---|
| ء | ʾ | د | d | ض | ḍ | ك | k |
| ب | b | ذ | dh | ط | ṭ | ل | l |
| ت | t | ر | r | ظ | ẓ | م | m |
| ث | th | ز | z | ع | ʿ | ن | n |
| ج | j | س | s | غ | gh | هـ | h |
| ح | ḥ | ش | sh | ف | f | و | w |
| خ | kh | ص | ṣ | ق | q | ي | y |

## Vowels

| | | | | | | |
|---|---|---|---|---|---|---|
| Short | ـَ | a | ـِ | i | ـُ | u |
| Long | ـَا | ā | ـِي | ī | ـُو | ū |
| Dipthongs | | ـَوْ | aw | ـَيْ | ay | |

| | |
|---|---|
| عَزَّوَجَلَّ | The Mighty and Majestic. |
| صَلَّىٱللَّهُعَلَيْهِوَسَلَّمَ | May Allāh make good mention of His Prophet in the highest company and grant him safety. |
| عَلَيْهِٱلسَّلَامُ | Peace be upon him. |
| رَضِيَٱللَّهُعَنْهُ | Allāh be pleased with him. |

**Note:** It is impossible to translate the Qurʾān into any other language whilst retaining its full range and depth of meaning. Hence, all verses from the Qurʾān cited in this work, whilst providing an accurate enough rendition of the basic meaning, remain limited due to the limitations of the English language and are unable to convey fully what is in the original Arabic.

# Foreword

All praise is due to Allāh,[1] the Creator and Lord of the Worlds, the Lord of Noah, Abraham, Moses, Jesus and Muḥammad. May the peace and blessings be upon them all.

The book in your hands is intended for:

- Non-Muslims interested in Islām or about to accept Islām;
- New Muslims who have just accepted Islām;
- Muslims wishing to learn or revise the basics;
- Parents desiring to familiarise their children with the basics.

This book serves all of these purposes at the same time and has been written with this goal in mind.

Utterance of the two testifications (shahādatān) regarding monotheism (tawḥīḍ) and messengership (risālah) enter a person into Islām. This declaration has a meaning (maʿnā), requirements (muqtaḍā), conditions (shurūṭ) and nullifiers (nawāqiḍ) which must be understood well. After a person enters Islām, he or she establishes the remaining pillars of Islām whilst seeking knowledge to increase inward Īmān, which is faith. This inevitably leads to righteous works, beneficial to the individual and the society. Thereafter, he or she strives for Iḥsān, which is the rank of excellence, and for perfection of morals and character. This was the purpose of the messengership of Muḥammad (ﷺ) who said: "*I was not sent [as a messenger] except to complete [perfect] the noble manners.*"[2]

Throughout the discussion of these subjects, important principles regarding belief and practice have been incorporated of which the reader must take note and learn. In addition, meanings and concepts have been simplified and explained through parables and analogies in order to facilitate better understanding. In sum, this work serves as both a primer on Islām and a concise revision guide.

Abū ʿIyāḍ Amjad Rafīq
27 Jumādā al-Thānī 1438 / 25 March 2017

---

[1] The name of this creator is Allāh (*īl, el, ilāh, iloh, elah*) in the languages of Hebrew, Aramaic (Syriac) and Arabic. This is not "*the God of the Muslims*" but the God of all Prophets, Messengers and mankind.

[2] Al-Bukhārī in *al-Adab al-Mufrad* and *al-Silsilah al-Ṣaḥīḥah* (no. 45).

# Introduction

Before we embark upon our discussion of the three levels which encompass Islām as a whole— and they are: Islām (submission), Īmān (faith) and Iḥsān (excellence)—there is some important background information that will help to set the context.

Modern research has established that belief in a creator is innate, hard-wired and natural. A creator's existence is also inferred from basic observation and reflection upon the natural phenomena in which there is order, regularity, beauty, adaptation, purpose and wisdom. This indicates **a purpose** to life. As such, the Creator would not neglect His creatures, but guide them to knowledge of their purpose and the means for its fulfilment. Thus, He sent Prophets with a message of **intrinsic meaning**, **value** and **direction** for human life. They explained the 'why' and the 'purpose' and conveyed moral codes and laws to enable the fulfilment of this purpose. Resurrection after death, accountability in the hereafter and recompense for one's deeds justify the affirmation of absolute morality and a right and wrong. This view of existence and life provides **a rational and coherent basis** for objective morality and produces *genuinely* (not *superficially*) happy people who have something to live for beyond the life of this world because it creates **constructive, optimistic feelings** through the anticipation of recompense, reward and justice for one's efforts, struggles and pains in this life.

This contrasts with the religious belief of atheists, naturalists and materialists that life is purely accidental and inherently meaningless and purposeless. This implies every human being is **insignificant** and **purposeless**. Thus, each person is born with the impossibility of ever knowing a 'why' or a 'purpose' and will be compelled to create his or her own meaning in life to avoid having nothing to live for.

This outlook tends to create **superficially happy people** with confused and contradictory ideas about what is right and wrong or moral and immoral. In this materialistic worldview, there is **no sound logical basis** for objective moral values and judgements. Thus, people can be easily and *justifiably* exploited morally, socially, economically and politically through philosophies and lifestyle systems devised by the shrewd and powerful. Some prominent atheists acknowledge that this view of life promotes **destructive, pessimistic feelings** in people when they realise that *ultimately*, *deep down* and in *actual reality*, their lives are utterly meaningless, worthless and purposeless.

Given that life has *intrinsic meaning and purpose*, the following five points explain how and why humans are responsible and accountable for their choices and actions:

**1. Faculties of knowledge and reflection**. The first point is that humans have been granted certain faculties which provide the basis for **personal responsibility** (taklīf) and **accountability** (ḥisāb). These faculties are:

- **hearing** (samʿ),
- **seeing** (baṣr),
- **feeling, reflecting and thinking** (fuʿād).

Allāh (عَزَّوَجَلَّ) said:

وَاللَّهُ أَخْرَجَكُم مِّن بُطُونِ أُمَّهَاتِكُمْ لَا تَعْلَمُونَ شَيْئًا وَجَعَلَ لَكُمُ السَّمْعَ وَالْأَبْصَارَ وَالْأَفْئِدَةَ لَعَلَّكُمْ تَشْكُرُونَ

"**And Allāh has brought you out from the wombs of your mothers while you knew nothing. And He gave you hearing, sight, and hearts that you might show gratitude.**" (16:78).

Through these basic faculties, a person observes phenomena that are contrived, regular, orderly and undeniably designed to facilitate and maintain life. They include the alternation of the night and day; the sun's light and life-giving qualities; the time-keeping of the sun and moon; the rain which revives the earth and brings forth its produce; the marvel of human reproduction; spouses which provide love and mercy to each other; the variation in skin complexions and languages; animals that provide food, transport and clothing; the abundance of plant varieties; the nourishment of water, honey, milk and so on. These phenomena work together in harmony comprising a sustenance-providing abode for its inhabitants in which they enjoy innumerable benefits. Humans are hard-wired to infer from these phenomena the presence of agency, and hence a creator.

In its entire history, humanity has never strayed from this innate, intuitive default, except after the spread of conjectural, pessimistic materialist philosophy over the past century or so. This hard-wiring is known as **fiṭrah** and includes a basic sense of purpose, common sense and morality which predisposes a person towards sound beliefs and beneficial actions. This is a raw, crude, malleable faculty and can be easily affected and moulded away from soundness to corruption during early childhood and beyond.

Thus, humans are endued with faculties (hearing, seeing, feeling and thinking) and an instinct, a default disposition which—coupled with the physical senses and reflection—make a person inclined towards belief in a creator and inculcate feelings of wanting to be grateful for the innumerable and indisputable favours he or she enjoys on a daily basis.

**2. Desiring and acting.** This leads us to the second point. There are two other faculties humans are endowed with: **desire, will** (irādah, mashīʾah) and **ability to act** (qudrah). A person is able to freely act on the basis of rational (or irrational) decisions—made possible through the aforementioned faculties of hearing, seeing and thinking—without feeling compelled. Allāh (عَزَّوَجَلَّ) said:

اعْمَلُوا مَا شِئْتُمْ إِنَّهُ بِمَا تَعْمَلُونَ بَصِيرٌ

"**Do whatever you will. Indeed, He is the seer of what you do**." (41:40). Thus, humans are able to acquire knowledge, think, reflect, evaluate, rationalise, desire, choose and act. This justifies the basis of human responsibility and accountability.

**3. Nurturing innate disposition to outward perfection.** Leading into the third point, the Creator sent revelation which cultivates the fiṭrah (whose likeness is that of a planted seed). Revelation leads it to outward perfection through sound knowledge (al-ʿilm al-nāfiʿ) and beneficial action (al-ʿamal al-ṣāliḥ). The famous Muslim scholar Ibn Taymiyyah (d. 1328) said: "The Messengers were sent in order to corroborate and perfect the innate disposition (fiṭrah)."[3] The nature of its perfection is indicated in the statement of the Prophet Muḥammad (صَلَّى ٱللَّهُ عَلَيْهِ وَسَلَّمَ), "*I was not sent [as a messenger] except to complete [perfect] the noble manners.*"[4] Thus, each soul, already innately inclined to worship its Creator, is invited towards inner and outer perfection through revealed knowledge which provides guidance and felicity and protection of one's beneficial interests in this life and the next.

---

[3] *Amrāḍ al-Qulūb wa Shifāʾuhā* (1402H, 3rd edition) p. 26.
[4] Al-Bukhārī in *al-Adab al-Mufrad* and *al-Silsilah al-Ṣaḥīḥah* (no. 45).

**4. Establishment of proof.** However, reward and punishment do not take place—and this is the fourth point— until and after **the proof has been established** (iqāmat al-ḥujjah). This takes place by way of the **revealed Books** (kutub) and **sent Messengers** (rusul).

Allāh (عَزَّوَجَلَّ) said:

رُّسُلًا مُّبَشِّرِينَ وَمُنذِرِينَ لِئَلَّا يَكُونَ لِلنَّاسِ عَلَى اللَّهِ حُجَّةٌ بَعْدَ الرُّسُلِ

"**[We sent] messengers as bringers of good tidings and warners so that mankind will have no argument against Allāh after the messengers.**" (4:165).

Detailed guidance, right and wrong, reward and punishment are not known except by way of revelation through the route of books and messengers. This revelation includes signs, proofs, evidences and rationalities which establish the truth of its message, the truthfulness of the Prophets and Messengers and the inevitability of resurrection, accountability and just recompense.

**5. No injustice.** Fifthly and finally, since humans have been given hearing, seeing, feeling and thinking, the ability to choose and act and have been shown right and wrong through books and messengers, Allāh's **justice** (ʿadl) has been established. Allāh is just in that he created humans already inclined towards His recognition and worship. He gave them faculties of sensory perception and reflection. He gave them the faculties of desiring, willing, choosing and effecting such desires and choices through their ability to act. He then sent Books and Messengers to direct them to clear, manifest signs and evidences which establish their truthfulness and the truth of what they convey. They conveyed guidance and made clear the path of truth, goodness and rectification from the paths of falsehood, evil and corruption. Thus, everyone who rejected and opposed the message cannot claim to have been wronged. Allāh's justice has already been established by virtue of what has preceded. From Allāh's justice is that He does not punish anyone—even if they are already committing wrong—until a messenger has been sent to them.

However, Allāh favours some of his creatures and gives them additional support in attaining guidance. It is given to those who sincerely desire it, yearn for it, seek it and pursue it.

وَيَزِيدُ اللَّهُ الَّذِينَ اهْتَدَوْا هُدًى

**"And Allah increases those who pursue and attain guidance, in [further] guidance.**" (19:76).

This is the **bounty and favour** (faḍl) of Allāh. Hence, all humans are in between either the justice of Allāh or the favour of Allāh. No one is wronged in this life, and none shall be wronged in the next when accountability, reward and punishment take place.

Allāh (عَزَّوَجَلَّ) said:

مَّنْ عَمِلَ صَالِحًا فَلِنَفْسِهِ وَمَنْ أَسَاءَ فَعَلَيْهَا وَمَا رَبُّكَ بِظَلَّامٍ لِّلْعَبِيدِ

**"Whoever does righteousness, it is for his own soul; and whoever does evil does so against it. And your Lord is never unjust to [His] servants.**" (41:46).

And He also said, which summarises the entire affair:

مَنِ اهْتَدَىٰ فَإِنَّمَا يَهْتَدِي لِنَفْسِهِ وَمَن ضَلَّ فَإِنَّمَا يَضِلُّ عَلَيْهَا وَلَا تَزِرُ وَازِرَةٌ وِزْرَ أُخْرَىٰ وَمَا كُنَّا مُعَذِّبِينَ حَتَّىٰ نَبْعَثَ رَسُولًا

**"Whoever pursues and attains guidance is only guided for [the benefit of] his soul. And whoever errs only errs against it. And no bearer of burdens will bear the burden of another. And never would We punish until We have sent a messenger.**" (17:15)

From these introductory points, it should become clear that **Allāh's justice** (ʿadl) has already been established with respect to you. From here, you are striving to attain **Allāh's favour** (faḍl) through the pursuit and attainment of right guidance which directs to beneficial knowledge and righteous action which in turn lead to perfection of morals and character, something every Muslim must strive for.

The Muslim scholar, Ibn al-Qayyim (d. 1350) said: "He, the Sublime, is the Just (al-ʿAdl) who does not transgress or oppress and whose servants do not fear oppression from Him. This is agreed upon by all of the Books and Messengers, and it is from the decisive [matters] in opposition to which no [revealed] legislation can bring anything and in opposition to which no Prophet can inform of anything, fundamentally."[5]

Ibn al-Qayyim also said: "Allāh, the Sublime—from the perfection of His mercy and benevolence—does not punish anyone except after

---

[5] *Hidāyat al-Ḥayārā*. Dār ʿĀlam al-Fawāʾid, p. 370.

sending a messenger to him, even if this person is already engaged in what deserves rebuke and punishment. Allāh has two proofs for His servant. Though He has prepared them, He will not punish him except after establishing them against him. The first of them is the innate disposition (fiṭrah) with which He created him and through which he innately affirms that [Allāh] is his Lord, Master and Originator and that His right is binding upon him.[6] And the second is the sending of His Messengers to him with a detailed elaboration of [what is already known by innate disposition], a corroboration and perfection of it. Hence, two witnesses will stand against him, **the witness of fiṭrah** and **the witness of legislation** [brought by a messenger]. And this person will bear witness against himself that he was a disbeliever, just as Allāh the Exalted said:

وَشَهِدُوا عَلَىٰ أَنفُسِهِمْ أَنَّهُمْ كَانُوا كَافِرِينَ

'**And they will bear witness against themselves that they were disbelievers.**' (6:130). Thus, He does not implement the judgement upon them except after corroboration by two witnesses and this is the extremity of justice."[7]

Let us then proceed to discuss the meaning of the testification which enters you into Islām, makes you sinless by wiping your slate clean and enters you into the mercy and forgiveness of Allāh, the most-Merciful, and His immense reward.

---

[6] In his Fixed-Point debate at the University of Alabama (2007), atheist Richard Dawkins admitted, "I think that when you consider the beauty of the world and you wonder how it came to be what it is, you are naturally overwhelmed with a feeling of awe, a feeling of admiration and you almost feel a desire to worship something. I feel this... We, all of us, share a kind of religious reverence for the beauties of the universe, for the complexity of life. For the sheer magnitude of the cosmos, the sheer magnitude of geological time. And it's tempting to translate that feeling of awe and worship into a desire to worship some particular thing, a person, an agent. You want to attribute it to a maker, to a creator." This is the fiṭrah, the innate disposition that everyone is born with. Disbelief (kufr) is to conceal, cover and prevent the fiṭrah from natural outward expression through one's pride, arrogance and preference for the world. Atheists do not have any empirical evidences for their claim that matter is eternal or that it self-creates and self-organises without choice and intent. It is pure conjecture.

[7] *Aḥkām Ahl al-Dhimmah*. Ramādī lil-Nashar (1418H) 2/1013-1014.

## The Meaning of 'Lā ilāha illallāh'

A person enters into Islām by uttering a testification (shahādah). By definition, testifying is to bear witness to something you know to be true and factual on the basis of direct experience.

The first part of the kalimah (statement of belief) is:

أشهد أن لا إله إلا الله

ash-hadu an lā ilāha illallāh

This means: "I testify that there is no deity [worthy of worship or worshipped in truth] except Allāh [alone]" and is explained by the following points:

**1. The meaning of ilāh (deity, god).** In Arabic, meanings of words are determined by their morphological patterns (shapes). The word ilāh takes the noun-pattern **fi'āl** (فِعَال), which is the same as **maf'ūl** (مَفْعُول), which means: *that to which something is done.* To illustrate: The word **kitāb** which takes this noun-pattern means book and a book is that which is written (**maktūb**), meaning, it was subject to the act of writing. Similarly, the word **bisāṭ** (rug) is that which is spread out (**mabsūṭ**), it was subject to spreading out. Similarly, the word **ilāh** which has the same pattern, translated as deity or god, is that which is subject to adoration and worship (**ma'lūh**). It is that in which people place and invest various states and feelings of the heart and make statements and perform actions amounting to veneration and worship. Thus, anything can be taken as a deity. Deities are numerous and diverse and can include both living and non-living things.

**2. A general negation (nafī).** The opening phrase of this sentence, "*Lā ilāha ...*" is a denial, a negation. It is a rejection **not** of the existence of other deities besides Allāh, since they are many, but of:

a) their worthiness of being taken as deities and worshipped,

b) their worship being truth (ḥaqq) and justice ('adl).

Hence, the first part of this phrase has the meaning that all deities erected and taken by men are not worthy of being taken as deities and do not deserve worship. That all deities worshipped are not worshipped in truth and justice, but in falsehood and injustice. This leads us to the second part of this phrase which is an exception to this generalisation.

**3. An affirmation (ithbāt) through exception.** The second part of the sentence, "... *illallāh*", is an exception to the general negation. It affirms that only Allāh, the Creator of the Heavens and Earth and whatever is in between is the true deity who is deserving and worthy of worship and whose worship comprises truth and justice. This is monotheism, singling out Allāh with worship and rejecting all other deities erected by men upon ignorance and injustice. It is known as the **unification of worship** (tawḥid al-ʿibādah). It is to unify all forms and types of worship for the one, true deity. Its proofs and evidences lie in His **evident lordship** over all of creation and His **beautiful names and lofty attributes** in which there is utmost perfection and in which He is resembled by none.

**4. Rational arguments for the tawḥīḍ of worship**. The Qurʾān outlines rational arguments for the truth of this statement—that none has the right to be worshipped but Allāh alone—and they can be summarised as follows:

- Evidence that no creature is able to **create** independently
- Evidence that no creature **owns** anything independently
- Evidence that no creature independently **regulates** the creation and this is know by the fact that it:
  - does not have independent control over life and death
  - does not have independent control over benefit and harm
  - does not have independent control over natural phenomena
  - does not have independent control over sustenance, provision
  - is not able to offer aid and deliver from calamities at will
  - is not able to guide others to the truth at will
  - is unable to hear, see and speak[8]
  - does not have independent knowledge of the unseen
  - is in need of food and drink and ultimately dies and perishes

In contrast, Allāh is the sole creator, the owner and regulator of His creation. He is the originator of all natural laws. He has absolute

[8] In the case of idols, statues and other inanimate deities.

control over benefit and harm, He hears, sees and speaks, is able to help, support, protect, deliver, guide and is not in need of food or drink. He is the ever-Living who never tires, sleeps or dies. This is indicative of His **unique, absolute lordship** (tawḥid al-rubūbiyyah). Thus, worshipping Him alone is truth and justice and worshipping other deities, in all their various forms, is falsehood and injustice.

**5. Beautiful names and lofty attributes.** In addition to the observed signs which indicate the lordship of Allāh and the rational evidences which establish the futility of worshipping other deities, what further establishes Allāh's unique, exclusive right to be worshipped is what He is described with of **names and attributes** (al-asmāʾ wal-ṣifāt).

By mere reflection alone, a person can arrive at a limited number of Allāh's attributes, such as knowledge, power, wisdom, will, love, mercy and generosity. However, the limits of observation and reason prevent the attainment of detailed and complete knowledge which can only be acquired through revelation from Allāh Himself. Allāh can only be spoken of and described through what He revealed about Himself as He is more knowledgeable of His own self. Speaking about Allāh without knowledge is a great sin and is severely prohibited. The Jews ascribed the defective attributes of humāns to Allāh and the Christians ascribed the divine attributes of Allāh to Jesus.

Allāh's attributes—unlike those of His creatures—are perfect and free of deficiencies. For example, Allāh hears and sees all things at all times. Hearing and seeing one does not preoccupy Him from hearing and seeing others. It is not within our knowledge or understanding to fathom how this can be, because we are only used to experiencing the limited, flawed hearing and seeing possessed by us and other creatures. This disparity between the perfect attributes of the creator and the flawed, limited attributes of the creation is another rational evidence that none has the right to be worshipped but Allāh alone.

Whilst there are shared attributes between the Creator and His creation, **the resemblance is in name (ism) and meaning (maʿnā) only**, not in the actual underlying **reality (ḥaqīqah)**. Without there being similarity in name and meaning, we would never be able to acquire any knowledge of Allāh through the medium of language. Thus, we would be unable to know and love Him. What is denied then is the similarity in the actual underlying realities and not the names and meanings. Thus, Allāh's knowledge is not like our knowledge, His hearing is not like our hearing, His love and mercy is not like our love and mercy and so on. This is because we have no knowledge of the reality of His essence and since the reality of attributes follows on from the reality of essences, we can never know the reality of His attributes. However, we understand the meanings of His attributes and this knowledge cultivates the heart with states and feelings that lead to the heart's love and yearning for its Lord.

Here are just some of the beautiful names of Allāh:

- **al-Aḥad**: The Unique
- **al-Raḥmān**: The Extremely Merciful.
- **al-Raḥīm**: The Bestower of mercy
- **al-A'lā**: The Most High
- **al-Akram**: The Most Generous.
- **al-Ilāh**: The One who alone deserves to be worshipped.
- **al-Awwal**: The First, before whom there is none.
- **al-Ākhir**: The Last, after whom there is none.
- **al-Ẓāhir**: The Uppermost One, lofty above all things.
- **al-Bāṭin**: The Innermost One, closest to all things.
- **al-Khallāq**: The Skilful Creator who creates again and again.
- **al-Bāri'**: The Maker
- **al-Fāṭir**: The Originator.
- **al-Ḥasīb**: The Reckoner who suffices.
- **al-Ḥamīd**: The Deservedly Praised.
- **al-Ḥayy**: The Ever Living who never dies.
- **al-Qayyūm**: The Self Subsisting upon whom everything depends.
- **al-Samī'**: The all-Hearing
- **al-Baṣīr**: The all-Seeing.
- **al-'Alīm**: The all-Knowing
- **al-Razzāq**: The Great Provider.
- **al-Shakūr**: The Most Ready to appreciate and reward abundantly.
- **al-Ṣamad**: The Perfect Master upon whom everything depends.
- **al-Qadīr**: The all-Powerful
- **al-Qāhir**: The Invincible Subduer.
- **al-Mutakabbir**: The Supreme in glory and justly proud.
- **al-Mujīb**: The Responsive to His slaves
- **al-Muqtadir**: The Omnipotent.

- **al-Muḥīt**: The All-encompassing from which nothing escapes.
- **al-Ra'ūf**: The Compassionate and Kind.
- **al-Raqīb**: The Ever Watchful Guardian.
- **al-Shahīd**: The Witness over all things.
- **al-'Azīz**: The Mighty and Invincible
- **al-Ghafūr**: The Oft-Forgiving.
- **al-Wakīl**: The Trustworthy disposer of affairs.

From the numerous attributes of Allāh are:

| | |
|---|---|
| - **life** (ḥayāt) | - **knowledge** ('ilm) |
| - **wish** (irādah) | - **power** (qudrah) |
| - **hearing** (sam') | - **seeing** (baṣr) |
| - **speech** (kalām) | - **mercy** (raḥmah) |
| - **love** (ḥubb) | - **wisdom** (ḥikmah) |
| - **majesty** (jalāl) | - **gentleness** (rifq) |
| - **majd** (glory) | - **honour** ('izzah) |

and many more.

A sound belief in this subject is summarised concisely through the following principles:

To affirm belief in Allāh's beautiful names and lofty attributes that are mentioned in His noble Book, the Qur'ān or have been mentioned by His noble Messenger (ﷺ) without:

a) distorting their wordings or meanings (taḥrīf),
b) denying them or divesting them from Allāh (ta'ṭīl),
c) likening their realities to those of His creatures (tamthīl),
d) specifying or asking how they are (takyīf).

It is obligatory to believe in the meaning of His attributes in a way that befits His Majesty without likening Him to His creation in any of His attributes and to believe that all of Allāh's attributes are perfect in every respect, without deficiencies.

The above can be summarised further in a more general, universal principle stated as: "Affirming His attributes (ithbāt) without making likenesses for them (tamthīl) and negating likeness for His attributes (tanzīḥ) without denying them (ta'ṭīl)."

The Muslim scholar Imām al-Sa'dī (d. 1956) said: "Every time a servant increases in his knowledge of the names of Allāh and His attributes, his faith and certainty increase."[9]

[9] *Al-Tawḍīh wal-Bayān Li Shajarat al-Īmān*. Aḍwā' al-Salaf. (1419H) p. 47.

It is upon a Muslim to acquaint himself with the names and attributes of Allāh, to understand their meanings, reflect upon them and then do what they require of speech and action. The Prophet (صَلَّى ٱللَّهُ عَلَيْهِ وَسَلَّمَ) said: "*To Allāh belong ninety-nine names, a hundred less one. Whoever learns [and acts upon them] will enter Paradise.*"[10] This refers to names which have been mentioned in the revealed texts, though Allāh's names are not limited to this number because He possesses unrevealed names that no one knows—not even the Prophets and Angels—except Him alone.

**6. Tawḥīd (monotheism).** Thus, the uniqueness of Allāh in His lordship—referred to as **tawḥid al-rubūbiyyah**—and the uniqueness of Allāh in His names and attributes—referred to as **tawḥid al-asmāʾ wal-ṣifāt**—are evidences that He alone is worthy of worship and that the worship of others besides Him is falsehood and in vain.

Hence, the central message of the Prophets, of all revealed books and of the Qurʾān is not that Allāh exists and that He alone creates, owns and regulates. This has never been disputed and is innately recognised by the overwhelming majority of humankind. Rather, the primary, central message of the Qurʾān contains the refutation of and warning against associating partners with Allāh in worship, which is falsehood and injustice, and the invitation to worship Allāh alone, which is truth and justice. Affirming Allāh's lordship—which has never been rejected by the vast majority of humanity—demands and necessitates only He is worshipped, exclusive to all other deities. This is the central argument of the Qurʾān against those who affirm belief in Allāh as Creator and Lord, but worship others besides Him.

However, over the passing of time throughout history humanity often strayed from innate disposition (fiṭrah) and reason (ʿaql) by erecting false deities through exaggeration of the status of righteous people, awe of the natural phenomena or veneration of the celestial bodies. False religion was built upon such exaggeration.

Allāh then sent messengers to guide them back to their original state of worshipping Allāh alone and shunning all false deities:

وَلَقَدْ بَعَثْنَا فِى كُلِّ أُمَّةٍ رَّسُولًا أَنِ ٱعْبُدُوا۟ ٱللَّهَ وَٱجْتَنِبُوا۟ ٱلطَّٰغُوتَ

[10] Reported by al-Bukhārī and Muslim from Abu Hurayrah (رَضِيَ ٱللَّهُ عَنْهُ).

"**And We have certainly sent into every nation a messenger, [saying], 'Worship Allāh [alone] and avoid false deities.**" (16:36).

**7. False deities.** A deity is only worshipped on the basis that it is able to provide some benefit. And a benefit can only be given by a being who possesses any one of four characteristics:

Either it is an **owner** (mālik) of whatever benefit the worshipper seeks from it. If not, then a **partner** (sharīk) in the ownership of the benefit being sought. If not, then an **assistant** (ẓahīr, muʿīn) of the owner of the benefit being sought. If not, then an **intercessor** (shafīʿ) who—without needing or obtaining permission—intercedes at will with the benefit's owner for the one seeking the benefit, regardless of whether the owner is pleased with the seeker or not.

Everything worshipped besides Allāh is worshipped on the basis of any one of these four false presumptions, all of which are negated and refuted in the Qur'ān:

قُلِ ٱدْعُوا۟ ٱلَّذِينَ زَعَمْتُم مِّن دُونِ ٱللَّهِ لَا يَمْلِكُونَ مِثْقَالَ ذَرَّةٍ فِى ٱلسَّمَٰوَٰتِ وَلَا فِى ٱلْأَرْضِ وَمَا لَهُمْ فِيهِمَا مِن شِرْكٍ وَمَا لَهُۥ مِنْهُم مِّن ظَهِيرٍ . وَلَا تَنفَعُ ٱلشَّفَٰعَةُ عِندَهُۥٓ إِلَّا لِمَنْ أَذِنَ لَهُۥ

"**Say, [O Muḥammad], 'Invoke those you claim [as deities] besides Allāh. They do not possess an atom's weight [of ability] in the Heavens or on the Earth, and they do not have therein any partnership [with Him], nor is there for Him from among them any assistant. And intercession does not benefit with Him except for one whom He permits'.**" (34:22-23).

By way of illustration, Abraham, Moses, Jesus (عَلَيْهِمُ السَّلَامُ) and Muḥammad (صَلَّى اللَّهُ عَلَيْهِ وَسَلَّمَ)—all lofty prophets amongst the Prophets of Allāh—do not own an atom's weight in the Heavens or Earth. Nor are they partners with Allāh in ownership. Nor are they helpers to Allāh in the running and regulation of the Heavens and Earth. Nor are they able to intercede with Allāh on behalf of anyone except after receiving permission to do so and only for one whose speech and deed Allāh is pleased with. When these four qualities are negated from rational, living beings, then that they should be negated from inanimate beings (stones, statues, idols, elements, forces) is greater in justification. Thus, the sun, the moon, stars, any of the natural phenomena, matter or energy in any of its forms, are not owners, partners in ownership, aiders or intercessors. Rather, they are owned by their creator, are subservient within the law-like behaviour determined for them and are subjected for goals, wisdoms and benefits. It is foolish to take anything from them as deities that are worshipped.

Hence, there is no rational basis for worshipping anything besides Allāh and worshipping other deities is falsehood, injustice and the height of foolishness, as Allāh (عَزَّوَجَلَّ) said:

وَمَن يَرْغَبُ عَن مِّلَّةِ إِبْرَاهِيمَ إِلَّا مَن سَفِهَ نَفْسَهُ

"**And who turns away from the religion of Abraham [the pure monotheist] except one who makes a fool of himself?**" (2:130).

**8. The Central Point of Dispute.** It should now be clear that the central point of dispute between the Messengers and the various people to whom they were sent was around the issue of worshipping Allāh alone, and not the mere belief that He exists and is the sole, unique creator, provider and sustainer. Every Messenger began his call by inviting his people to single out Allāh in worship and to abandon worship of all other deities; this forming the basis for an upright, just, moral, genuinely happy and prosperous society. In the Qurʾān, every Messenger is recorded as having said to his people:

يَا قَوْمِ اعْبُدُوا اللَّهَ مَا لَكُم مِّنْ إِلَٰهٍ غَيْرُهُ

"**O my people! Worship Allāh alone, you have no other deity besides Him.**" (7:65).

However, the leaders of the people—those who control, influence and direct them—had vested interests in the various deities that had been erected and these interests were social, economic and political in nature, relating to wealth, status and power. Unwilling to let go of these interests, despite knowing the truth of what the Messengers called to, these people showed opposition, enmity and aggression towards the Messengers and their followers. The Messengers were accused of being liars, magicians, insane, trouble-causers and their followers were ridiculed as being unintelligent, lowly, weak and poor. Allāh (عَزَّوَجَلَّ) said regarding these leaders and influencers:

وَعَجِبُوٓاْ أَن جَآءَهُم مُّنذِرٌ مِّنْهُمْ وَقَالَ ٱلْكَٰفِرُونَ هَٰذَا سَٰحِرٌ كَذَّابٌ. أَجَعَلَ ٱلْآلِهَةَ إِلَٰهًا وَٰحِدًا إِنَّ هَٰذَا لَشَىْءٌ عُجَابٌ. وَٱنطَلَقَ ٱلْمَلَأُ مِنْهُمْ أَنِ ٱمْشُواْ وَٱصْبِرُواْ عَلَىٰٓ ءَالِهَتِكُمْ إِنَّ هَٰذَا لَشَىْءٌ يُرَادُ

**"And they wonder that there has come to them a warner from among themselves. And the disbelievers say, 'This is a magician and a liar. Has he made the gods [only] one God? Indeed, this is a curious thing.' And the eminent (the leaders) among them went forth, [saying], 'Continue, and remain constant over [worship and defence of] your gods. Indeed, this is a thing desired.** (38:4-7).

The disbelievers also exulted in the advanced worldly knowledge they possessed, wrongly thinking it made them superior and justified their rejection of the Messengers and what they called to:

فَلَمَّا جَاءَتْهُمْ رُسُلُهُم بِالْبَيِّنَاتِ فَرِحُوا بِمَا عِندَهُم مِّنَ الْعِلْمِ

**"Then when their Messengers came to them with clear proofs, they were glad (and proud) with that which they had of the knowledge (of worldly things).**" (40:83).

Hence, the battle was around the issue of worshipping Allāh alone (tawḥīd) and shunning all other deities *because* it is liberation from enslavement. The leaders of the people knew and understood the *social*, *economic* and *political* implications of people leaving invented, fabricated gods and worshipping the only true deity, submitting to Allāh alone.[11] Whoever claims that the Messengers came to simply establish *belief in a supreme creator* and that this was the nature of their monotheistic call, is in plain, manifest error.

---

[11] A Muslim who worships Allāh alone and takes his guidance, morals and law from Islām does not deal with usury (interest). He does not drink. He does not gamble. He does not engage in fornication before marriage or adultery after it. All of these are destroyers of society. They lead to loss of life and intellect; destruction and embezzlement of wealth; economic enslavement through debt burden; disruption of lineage; breakdown of marriage and its abolition as an institution; removal of material (private property) and inheritance rights and so on. A Muslim woman guards her modesty and chastity and is not exploitable, economically or socially. Thus, Muslims, as a commodity, are not as profitable and do not make good, exploitable slaves. Islām leads to rectification of societies and is a hindrance to private interests founded on exploitation of base human desires.

**9. The meaning of the testification.** Thus, in light of all that has preceded, with this simple concise statement, *Lā ilāha illallāh*, you are expressing the following truthful, profound, powerful, liberating, enriching and self-empowering meaning:

"I have firm knowledge and conviction—arrived at by innate disposition, sensory perception, common sense, rational evidences and sound reason guided by revelation—of the fact that there is no deity except that it is worshipped in falsehood and injustice, not truth and justice, whether this deity is inanimate (stones, statues, idols) or animate (trees, animals, humans, angels, jinn), or from the observed phenomena (sun, moon, wind, rain, lightning, thunder) or any of the natural laws or cause-effect mechanisms within creation (interplays of matter, energy, forces). That none of these entities or forces are worthy of being worshipped because they are mere slaves, subject to laws and do not have independent powers to create, own, regulate, guide, misguide, aid, rescue and so on. The only deity worthy of worship and who is worshipped in truth and justice is Allāh, the Creator of the Heavens and Earth, creator of all beings, of all elements and forces and of all natural laws and cause-effect mechanisms, the One described with the most beautiful names and the loftiest attributes, the ever-Living who never dies."

The Prophet Muḥammad (ﷺ) said: "*Whoever said 'Lā ilāha illallāh' sincerely from his heart will enter Paradise.*"[12] He also ordered one of his companions, Abū Hurayrah (رَضِيَ ٱللَّٰهُ عَنْهُ), to give glad tidings of Paradise to "*the one who testifies that none has the right to be worshipped but Allāh whilst having firm conviction in his heart.*"[13] These statements are for the who expresses this statement with sincerity and firm conviction and thereafter abides by its requirements in speech and deed, remains firm upon it and dies upon it.

**10. The greatest injustice.** It should now be clear that the greatest injustice is to associate partners with Allāh in worship. The worship of others—whether humans, the jinn, the angels, the celestial bodies including the earth, sun and moon, the elements, trees, stones, even

[12] *Ṣaḥīḥ al-Jāmiʿ al-Ṣaghīr* (no. 6433) and *al-Silsilah al-Ṣaḥīḥah* (no. 2355).
[13] Related in Kitāb al-Īmān in *Ṣaḥīḥ Muslim.*

the prophets themselves or the righteous living or dead or the elements and forces—is the greatest injustice (ẓulm). In Islāmic terminology it is referred to as **associationism** (shirk) and is the only sin that will never be forgiven if a person dies upon it:

إِنَّ اللَّهَ لَا يَغْفِرُ أَن يُشْرَكَ بِهِ وَيَغْفِرُ مَا دُونَ ذَٰلِكَ لِمَن يَشَاءُ وَمَن يُشْرِكْ بِاللَّهِ فَقَدِ افْتَرَىٰ إِثْمًا عَظِيمًا

"**Verily, Allāh forgives not that partners should be set up with him in worship, but He forgives besides that [anything else] to whom He pleases. And whoever sets up partners with Allāh in worship, has indeed invented a tremendous sin.**" (4:48).

This crime is more unjust than stealing, murder, adultery and other similar crimes and transgressions which, although serious, can be forgiven. These crimes are crimes of desires, lusts and passions and are not driven by rejection of the universal order. As for *shirk*, it is a gross violation of the universal order.

Its reality can be highlighted through the example of a person who shows gratitude and devotion to a tree, brick, mouse or cat for the many years of toil and struggle that his parents endured in raising him.[14] Or the example of when someone charitably builds a house for another and this person gives thanks and appreciation to the wood, bricks and cement of the completed house rather than to the builder of the house.

This is raw foolishness, a violation of the empirically known order of things and gross injustice. In a similar way, worshipping humans—including the prophets and the righteous, dead or alive—animals, the forces, the elements or anything from the intertwined system of causes and effects within this universe is gross injustice. It opposes innate disposition and comprises revilement of sound intellect.

[14] This is not to imply that the Creator of the Heavens and the Earth becomes weary or tired in maintaining and providing for His creatures. He (عَزَّوَجَلَّ) said regarding the Heavens and Earth, "**Their preservation tires Him not. And He is the Most High, the Most Great**" (2:255). Allāh (عَزَّوَجَلَّ) provides and spends upon His creatures without anything diminishing from His kingdom and without any tiredness or weariness on His behalf, He is the ever-living (al-Ḥayy) sustainer (al-Qayyūm) of all things. Nothing is diminished from His dominion by providing for His creatures.

The Qurʾānic reasoning against those who worship other deities is clear, simple and powerful: How can you affirm that Allāh:[15]

- is the Creator of the Heavens, the Earth, and all of humanity
- subjected the sun and moon (for humanity 's benefit)
- sends down rain and revives the Earth
- owns the dominion of the Earth and of all things
- has the most beautiful names and lofty attributes
- is the Lord of the Seven Heavens and of the Mighty Throne
- is sought for refuge and there is no refuge from Him
- sustains creation through provisions from Heaven and Earth
- bestows and controls faculties of sight and hearing
- brings living out of the dead and the living out of the dead
- regulates, controls all of the creation
- responds to the one in distress when he invokes Him

and yet you worship others besides Him, when they do not have any of these qualities or perform any of these actions. Some of you sincerely worship Allāh alone during calamities when you know none can save but He, but worship others during times of ease. Even worse, some of you worship others in times of both hardship and ease!

Hence, such people are rebuked severely in the Qurʾān through the statements: "**How are they deluded?**" (29:61), "**How are they bewitched?**" (23:89), "**They do not take admonition!**" (23:85), "**They do not have piety, fear of Allāh!**" (23:87).

**11. Doubts and misconceptions.** There are associationists (mushriks) who ascribe to Islām but have followed the ways of previous nations. They have arguments to justify their worship of other deities. They claim to believe firmly in Allāh's Lordship yet invoke saints to solicit their intercession, claiming that the saints have status with Allāh and can petition Allāh on their behalf. They also invoke them for rescue, claiming Allāh responds to them when they invoke the saints. They wrongly assert that these actions of invocation and calling for rescue [in affairs which only Allāh has power over] do not constitute

---

[15] One can refer to the following verses in the Qurʾān: Luqmān (31:25), al-Zumar (39:38), al-ʿAnkabūt (29:61), al-Zukhruf (43:87), al-ʿAnkabut (29:63), al-Zukhruf (43:9), al-Muʾminūn (23:84-89) and Yunus (10:31).

worship, though they are the greatest forms of worship. Hence, they misunderstand the reality and nature of worship (ʿibādah).

Further, they try to differentiate the worship of saints from the worship of idols despite the fact that in the Qurʾān, Allāh *did not differentiate between any of the numerous categories worshipped besides Him*, whether the sun, moon, stars, stones, idols, humans, prophets, angels or the jinn. The **core, central issue** is giving *anything or anyone* a share of worship that is due to Allāh alone, irrespective of what or who that thing is. The sum of these doubts and misconceptions can be addressed by the following points:

a) Those to whom the Prophet (ﷺ) was sent did not dispute that Allāh is the Lord, the Creator, the Owner and Provider. They had firm, unwavering conviction in this as is evident in the Qurʾān, as has already preceded, and this did not enter them into Islām.

b) The various factions addressed by the Qurʾān include those who worship the sun, moon, stars, stones, idols, trees, angels, jinn and the prophets and righteous. The Qurʾān did not distinguish between any of them, because they all directed something of worship—such as invocation (duʿā)—to other than Allāh.

c) Their argument was that they certainly do not affirm lordship for their deities, nor do they directly ask their deities to repel harm and bring benefit. But rather, they simply desire the **intercession** of those whom they invoke and seek **nearness** to Allāh through them.

d) From the above, it should be clear that associationism (shirk) is not limited to idols or the worship of inanimate things alone. The Qurʾān refutes not just the idol-worshippers, but a variety of factions including those who invoke the Prophets and righteous.

e) Those who worship idols do not believe that their idols create, own and regulate anything. No idol-worshipper ever believed such a thing. Idols are used as **focal points** for the original entity being worshipped: a celestial body, a heavenly spirit or a human being amongst other things. This worship is justified by the claim that to approach Allāh *indirectly* through intermediaries is better than to approach Him directly. The Qurʾān and all revealed Books came to invalidate this falsehood as it is the foundation of associationism.

f) Invoking the prophets and the righteous is indeed worship even if one does not believe that they create, own or regulate. Invocation (duʿā) is from the greatest forms and types of worship and is given much attention in the Qurʾān. The Qurʾānic prohibition of invoking others besides Allāh is explicit:

فَلَا تَدْعُوا مَعَ اللَّهِ أَحَدًا

"**So invoke not, anyone alongside Allāh.**" (72:18).

Just as the command to invoke Him alone is explicit:

فَادْعُوا اللَّهَ مُخْلِصِينَ لَهُ الدِّينَ

"**So invoke Allāh making worship purely for Him alone.**" (40:14).

Hence, invocation (duʿā) is worship. To invoke others—*irrespective of whether one believes that they create, own and regulate or not*—amounts to worship. Further, if a person truly believed that Allāh alone creates, owns and regulates, then he or she would not invoke others. This is a clear contradiction between what one believes and what one does. The entire argument of the Qurʾān in affirmation of Tawḥīd and invalidation of associationism is against this blatant contradiction.

**13. Safeguarding Tawḥīd.** Since Tawhīd is the most excellent of good deeds and since its opposite, associationism is the worst of evil deeds, then the Qurʾān and the Prophetic traditions, representing complete guidance, have ensured that *all avenues leading to the creation of false deities and worship of them besides or alongside Allāh* are cut off **at their roots**. Hence, the following affairs (by way of example) are enjoined in the texts and should be observed:

§ Having the utmost sincerity and truthfulness in one's intentions, words and deeds.

§ Not excessively praising and raising people above their levels, including the prophets and righteous.

§ Not raising, adorning and embellishing graves.

§ Not imitating the ways of previous nations whose excesses and innovations led them to worship others besides Allāh.

§ Not building mosques in graveyards or making gravesites as places where Allāh is worshipped.

§ The prohibition of astrology and the futility of the claim that the celestial bodies and their positions and movements affect life, death, victory, defeat, fortune and misfortune.

§ Prohibition of charms, talismans and amulets.

§ Prohibition of praying during sunset and sunrise to avoid the presumption that the sun is being worshipped.

§ Not creating statues of humans and animals or any other form of representation as this can lead, over time, to their veneration and deification. Thus, the route is cut off from the very beginning.[16]

§ The prohibition of belief in omens wherein negative effects are wrongly believed to be tied to certain causes, leading to baseless fear and undue abandonment of desirable activities.

§ Severe prohibition of magic as it is a doorway to associationism (shirk) and disbelief (kufr).

For the sake of brevity, we have mentioned only some of the many affairs a person should know and be cautious of. However, a person must make a detailed study of this important subject matter and not remain ignorant about it, as ignorance leads to misguidance. Allāh has prohibited all ways and means that lead to deities being erected and worshipped. He has also command all the ways and means that safeguard a person's Tawḥīd in belief, speech and deed.

**14. Deviation from Tawḥīd occurs in small steps.** Satan is an avowed enemy to the offspring of Ādam (عَلَيْهِ السَّلَامُ). He refused to obey Allāh's command to prostrate to Ādam out of pride and arrogance and when doomed to punishment, he asked for respite which he was given till the Day of Judgement. **He then promised to mislead all the children of Ādam by making them become ungrateful, worship others alongside Allāh and do deeds opposed to their original nature, deeds that are harmful to themselves and to society**. He has done this throughout history—using a step by step method that usually spans many generations—thereby giving rise to false religion which takes on many forms and manifestations. The Prophet (صَلَّى ٱللَّهُ عَلَيْهِ وَسَلَّمَ) said, relating that Allāh (عَزَّ وَجَلَّ) said: "*Indeed, I created My servants upright, inclined to truth. But then the devils came to them and caused them to swerve from their religion [of monotheism].*"[17] Allāh sent Messengers to humanity to guide them and return them to their original state.

---

[16] Muslim scholars make exceptions for matters of necessity such as passports, driving licences, identity cards and what is similar.

[17] Related by Muslim in his Ṣaḥīḥ (no. 5109).

From the cunning of Satan is that he misguides through small unnoticeable steps and his schemes lasts many generations, over hundreds of years. He takes human beings either from the angle of *excess and exaggeration* or the angle of *belittlement and neglect*.

We will provide an illustration as to how Satan uses exaggeration (ghuluww) in righteous people to lead people into worshipping them as deities alongside Allāh. This will also reveal the wisdoms of the Qur'ānic and Prophetic teachings in cutting off all the routes through which people might deviate from the Tawḥīd of the Messengers.

**The First Step:** When a righteous figure dies Satan, knowing of the great respect and love people have for this person, inspires the close relatives of the deceased—through their love of the deceased and their desire to respect and honour the deceased—to embellish the grave and build over it. People compete with each other in this regard, thinking that they are showing greater respect and honour to their loved ones over others and that not doing so entails disrespect and belittlement of the deceased.

**The Second Step:** Beautification of graves requires maintenance, leading to frequent visits to the grave. During these visits, Satan inspires a person with the idea that invoking Allāh (عَزَّوَجَلَّ) by the grave is commendable, if not better than invoking Him at home or the mosque, and that it is more likely to be responded to.

**The Third Step:** Over time, the person moves from invoking Allāh directly by the side of the grave to invoking Allāh through the dead person in the form of asking Allāh for his needs by mentioning the status (jāh) or right (ḥaqq) of the dead person. He says, "O Allāh I ask you by the right this person has with you" or "I ask you by the status this person has with you". Satan inspires this person to wrongly believe that Allāh must answer his invocation with mere mention of the status or right of the deceased and this is disrespect to Allāh, it is a type of imposition, as if Allāh must respond. Allāh is not obliged to respond to a person merely because of the good standing of another. The two affairs are unconnected and Allāh did not legislate this approach as a fruitful means. Whilst this act in itself is not associationism (shirk) because the deceased has not yet been invoked and worshipped directly, it is a stepping stone towards it.

**The Fourth Step:** Once a person has been accustomed to invoking Allāh and requesting from Him through the status of the deceased, it is a natural step to invoke the deceased directly and ask for his or her intercession (shafāʿah) with Allāh. Satan inspires this person to believe that the deceased can hear and respond, first from near and then from afar. Rather than remain within the limits of guidance and patience and suffice himself with his own invocation and that of the living for him, he reasons that the dead person is closer to Allāh (due to his piety and because he is in the intermediate stage between the world and the hereafter). He therefore asks the deceased—as an intermediate intercessor— to invoke Allāh (عَزَّوَجَلَّ) on his behalf and ask Allāh for the fulfilment of his needs, whether attaining some good or repelling some harm. He may address the deceased directly by first standing at his grave, and then later from a distance, away from the grave. At this point, associationism (shirk) has occurred because this person is now clearly directing worship (invocation) to the deceased.

**The Fifth Step:** Satan then inspires him to believe that winning favour with the deceased helps him to earn continuous intercession from him with Allāh and therefore, he must venerate and respect the deceased through acts of devotion. It is here that the deceased and his grave will be taken as an idol worshipped alongside Allāh and the door is opened for all other major acts of worship to be directed to the deceased: seeking rescue in times of hardship (istighāthah), seeking aid in matters which only Allāh has power over (istiʿānah), asking for cure, making a devotional sacrifice of an animal (dhabh) and so on. Satan inspires such people to believe that this is the right of the deceased, to be venerated and respected in this manner and that their worldly affairs will not be set aright without this.

**The Sixth Step:** Then Satan inspires the leaders amongst them to call the people at large to this way. He commands them to make the graves and tombs of the deceased as celebratory locations (ʿīd) and places of devotion which are most beneficial for them in this life and the next. He incites them to rush to these locations for the fulfilment of their needs. By now, the foundations of false religion have been laid down. Many forms of social and economic exploitation naturally follow. A *religious system* develops and allows for some to enrich themselves through the exploitation of the ignorant, naive and gullible and those looking for cheap salvation without having to bear the burden of observing the law. The beneficiaries of false religion then show enmity to anyone who calls for invocation and worship to be made only to Allāh and who expounds the Tawḥīd of the Messengers, that none has the right to be worshipped but Allāh alone and who explains that respecting the deceased does not mean granting them a right which belongs only to Allāh (عَزَّوَجَلَّ). Rather, one invokes Allāh's forgiveness for them as they are most in need of that whilst they are not invoked alongside Him. Yet the associationists claim that this is belittlement and disrespect of the righteous dead and constitutes war against Allāh because the righteous dead are His close allies and friends (awliyāʾ). They argue that *not fulfilling their rights* (they mean: *to invoke and worship them*) is the greatest of crimes. The leaders incite the common folk against the callers to truth, deceiving them into thinking that the callers to Tawḥīd are the enemies of Allāh, when in reality they are His friends and allies.

Thus, the deception becomes complete and Satan has successfully misguided them through his cunning, step by step, just as he did with the people of Noah (عَلَيْهِ السَّلَامُ) and many nations throughout history. Not only did he misguide them, but he made them his soldiers in inviting to disbelief (kufr) and associationism (shirk). In such a manner, Satan made false religion fair-seeming to great multitudes of people across the Earth and made Islām—whenever a messenger or his followers called to it—to appear strange and backward.

The above discussion also highlights the nature of idol-worship. It is in fact a nexus, a web of many things. Underlying it is veneration and worship of celestial bodies, spirits or humans while physical objects are used as focal points to channel devotion to these deities.

The Qurʾān addresses all aspects and elements of this web.

**In summary:** Through the above, we should have acquired a thorough understanding of the first part of the declaration of Islām which is centred around Tawḥīd, which is to single out Allāh in worship exclusive to all other deities.

Let us proceed to the second part relating to messengership which is the means by which knowledge of how the first is actualised is acquired, there being no other way to acquire this knowledge.

## The Meaning of 'Muḥammad Rasūlullāh'

The second part of the statement of belief (kalimah) is:

وأشهد أن محمدا رسول الله

wa ash-hadu anna muḥammadan rasūlullāh

This means: "And I testify that Muḥammad is the Messenger of Allāh" and is explained by general points followed by specific points. As for the general:

1. **Belief in the Prophets and Messengers.** Prophet Muḥammad (صَلَّى ٱللَّهُ عَلَيْهِ وَسَلَّمَ) is the last in a series of messengers starting with Noah (عَلَيْهِ ٱلسَّلَامُ). All of them called to Islām upon the foundation of pure monotheism as has preceded. Testifying to the messengership of Muḥammad (صَلَّى ٱللَّهُ عَلَيْهِ وَسَلَّمَ) incorporates belief in all previous prophets and messengers. Rejecting any previous prophet sent by Allāh is a rejection of prophethood in principle. Similarly, rejecting the prophethood of Muḥammad (صَلَّى ٱللَّهُ عَلَيْهِ وَسَلَّمَ) is a rejection of all previous prophets including Noah, Abraham, Moses and Jesus (عَلَيْهِمُ ٱلسَّلَامُ) and of prophethood itself. Hence, this second part of the testification affirms both the prophethood of Muḥammad (صَلَّى ٱللَّهُ عَلَيْهِ وَسَلَّمَ) and of all previous prophets by inclusion. The Islām of Muḥammad (صَلَّى ٱللَّهُ عَلَيْهِ وَسَلَّمَ) is a perfection of the Islām of all previous prophets. The Prophets and Messengers are the route through which tawḥīd and its details are acquired and learned. Thus, the binding link between **monotheism** (tawḥīd) and **messengership** (risālah).

2. **Intermediaries of conveyance, not worship.** The Prophet Muḥammad (صَلَّى ٱللَّهُ عَلَيْهِ وَسَلَّمَ) and all other prophets and messengers were **intermediaries of conveyance (bulūgh)** only. They simply conveyed the revelations of Allāh and did so with integrity. They faithfully performed the duty they were entrusted with. They taught beneficial knowledge and righteous action whilst giving people glad tidings and warnings. They were upright, truthful, noble, ethical and moral men who did not fall into major sins. They are not intermediaries who are worshipped or through whom worship is channelled to Allāh. They do not possess any divine attributes, nor did they call people to

worship them. The Christians have lied who claim Jesus (عَلَيهِ السَّلَام) called to his own worship or to the worship of his mother Mary (عَلَيهَا السَّلَام). Jesus will declare himself innocent of their worship and repudiate them on the Day of Reckoning. Likewise, they have lied who ascribed repugnant things to the Prophets and Messengers.[18]

**3. Obedience to the messengers.** The Prophets and Messengers were sent to be obeyed, their obedience being commanded by Allāh and entailing obedience to Allāh Himself:

وَمَا أَرْسَلْنَا مِن رَّسُولٍ إِلَّا لِيُطَاعَ بِإِذْنِ اللَّهِ

"**We sent no Messenger, but to be obeyed by Allāh's Leave.**"(4:64). And also:

مَّن يُطِعِ الرَّسُولَ فَقَدْ أَطَاعَ اللَّهَ

"**He who obeys the Messenger has obeyed Allāh.**" (4:80)

Hence, the Prophets and Messengers are obeyed in what they command and forbid because everything they convey of revelation, guidance, commands and prohibitions originates with Allāh and does not originate from themselves.

**4. Chosen, not philosophers.** The Prophets and Messengers are not philosophers or merely shrewd, wise men with strong sensory perception coupled with creative imaginations and strong leadership qualities. Rather, they are **chosen and honoured** by Allāh to convey His message. Prophethood cannot be earned or acquired, it is only

---

[18] As for the negative portrayal of the Prophets of Allāh in the Torah and the ascription of reprehensible deeds to them, then all of it comes from the fabrications of the poisoned pens of the scribes. All the Prophets and Messengers were noble, upright, righteous men. They were infallible in matters of revelation and its conveyance. They were secure (maʿṣūm) from falling into major sin. As for minor sins (errors), the Prophets may fall into them, but they do not persist upon them after being notified by Allāh and repenting. Further, Prophets and Messengers have a much higher standard of uprightness in character than those besides them. Thus, their "minor sins" may comprise of mistakes and errors in judgement—such as choosing the least beneficial of two beneficial options—for which an ordinary person would not be blamed. This is the Islāmic position regarding the status of the Prophets and Messengers.

bestowed. The divine guidance of the Prophets and Messengers is superior to the speculations and ramblings of the philosophers which generally tend to be their own subjective views strongly shaped and determined by their personal experiences. The unified, coherent message of all the Prophets and Messengers and the incoherence and contradiction both between and within the views of philosophers is an indication of their ignorance and misguidance.

The effect and influence of the teachings of the Prophets and Messengers are unequalled and unrivalled by anything put forth by the philosophers. The mention of the Messengers, such as Noah, Abraham, Moses, Jesus (عَلَيْهِمُ السَّلَامُ) and Muḥammad (صَلَّى ٱللَّهُ عَلَيْهِ وَسَلَّمَ) has been made great among the nations, and of them Muḥammad (صَلَّى ٱللَّهُ عَلَيْهِ وَسَلَّمَ) is the most remembered and praised, indicating the truth of his name, which means "the praised one". **John William Draper**, (d. 1882), an American scientist and historian, wrote: "Four years after the death of Justinian, A.D. 569, was born at Mecca, in Arabia, the man who, of all men, exercised the greatest influence upon the human race... Moḥammed."[19]

And as for the specific points:

**1. The Messengership of Muḥammad (صَلَّى ٱللَّهُ عَلَيْهِ وَسَلَّمَ).** Muḥammad[20] (صَلَّى ٱللَّهُ عَلَيْهِ وَسَلَّمَ) is the son of ʿAbdullāh, the son of ʿAbd al-Muṭṭālib, the son of Hāshim and his lineage traces back, through 21 generations, to ʿAdnān who was from the offspring of Ishmael, the son of Abraham. He was sent at a time when the teachings and traces of previous messengers had either been lost or distorted. The pagans of Arabia had inherited many of the deities of the ancients and worshipped them alongside Allāh. The Sabeans worshipped the celestial bodies. The Jews and Christians had departed from the teachings of Moses and Jesus respectively (عَلَيْهِمَا السَّلَامُ) and altered their religion through

---

[19] "*A History of the Intellectual Development of Europe*", 1875, vol.1, pp. 329-330. Draper's view is also expressed by others who list the Prophet as the most influential man in history, above all other famous people, be they kings, philosophers, leaders, reformists, scientists or religious figures.

[20] The name 'Muḥammad' means *the praised one* and *as a matter of fact* he is the most mentioned and praised person on Earth, ever.

distortion of their revealed books and the accumulation of concepts and beliefs from other nations. All other nations had likewise fallen into the worship of other deities besides or alongside Allāh.

From the start of his prophethood in 610 CE and for a period of 13 years in Mecca, the Prophet preached peacefully to the pagan Arabs who held a variety of beliefs. He invited them to single out Allāh in worship and shun the worship of deities that have no power over benefit or harm. He spoke against their racism, their maltreatment of slaves, killing of female newborns and other misdeeds. He enjoined benevolence to widows and orphans and the frequent giving of charity. Unfortunately, his message was not in the personal, economic and political interests of the pagans of Mecca. He was shown hostility and his believing companions were oppressed, tortured and murdered. Attempts were made on his life and he was forced to migrate to what became known as the city of Madīnah in 622 CE. He continued preaching for another ten years whilst facing hostility, plots and the machinations of the polytheists and various forces who formed alliances and initiated wars against him.

Being granted permission to ward off aggression and injustice from himself and his believing companions, he only fought to defend the instrument of peaceful preaching so that the message of Islām, genuine monotheism and perfection of morals and character, could be heard by others without any hindrance. He never forced a single person to accept Islām against his will. He invited the Jews back to the religion of Prophet Moses (عَلَيْهِ ٱلسَّلَامُ). Through the Qurʾān, they were reminded of their past: how they were favoured when they adhered to right guidance and how their leaders departed from that guidance, opposed their Prophets, distorted their book, entered into magic and the occult and other iniquities. He also argued with the Christians and invited them back to the religion of Prophet Jesus (عَلَيْهِ ٱلسَّلَامُ). He explained to them that Jesus was not divine, never claimed to be and never asked to be worshipped. He explained that Jesus called to the worship of the one true deity, Allāh, and none other, and that his mother was a chaste, truthful, righteous woman who was favoured and honoured by Allāh.

Despite many wars waged to extinguish his message, the Prophet came out victorious and the entire Arabian peninsula entered Islām during the last two years of his prophethood, willingly and without compulsion. His followers were victorious over the great nations of the time, the Romans and Persians. Islām eventually spread all the way to westernmost Africa, reaching France and Switzerland on one side of the Earth and northern Australia on the other side.[21]

**2. Proofs of prophethood**. The proofs of the prophethood of Muḥammad (ﷺ) are many, diverse and not restricted to any one particular matter. Prior to his prophethood he was known to his people as 'the truthful and trustworthy' (al-ṣādiq wal-amīn). He had an impeccable, lofty character, a matter acknowledged by many non-Muslim writers and historians who praised him.[22]

An objective, unbiased study and analysis of his biography, his character and his dealings with friend and foe alike will indicate his truthfulness. When one gathers and analyses his **information** (khabar), **command** (amr), **prohibition** (nahī), **speech** (qawl) and **deed** (fiʿl), there is complete coherence in all of it. An imposter is very quickly exposed through what he informs of, commands, prohibits, says and does. It is not possible for a liar or imposter to maintain honesty, integrity and coherence in all of these five fields without his reality becoming known through interaction with others. Rather, his lies and contradictions would quickly become apparent to people. Hence, the character of Muḥammad (ﷺ), from these various aspects, is the strongest of evidences—aside from the Qurʾān—of his prophethood.

He was granted many miracles which have been reported by large-scale successive transmission through honest and trustworthy reporters and subsequently documented. These reports outnumber and overwhelm the reports of the miracles of previous prophets.

His victory and that of his initial small number of followers over sizeable aggressive enemies and against the most powerful nations of the time, the Romans and Persians, is proof of divine aid. If he had

---

[21] The spread of Islām, unlike European Christian colonialism, was not accompanied by wholesale extermination of indigenous people.

[22] A number of non-Muslim historians (such as John William Draper whose citation has preceded) described Muḥammad (ﷺ) as the most *influential* man in the whole of history.

been an imposter or a liar, he would not have been given aid and granted such success. It is not possible for the one who knows he is lying and deceiving others to possess an iron-strong determination and firm resolve without doubting, wavering, faltering and giving up.

His prophecies—numbering in the hundreds—regarding future events and signs which occurred and took place just as he mentioned are also a proof of his truthfulness.

Consideration of his legislation—which protects the necessities of life, property, lineage, honour and intellect and saves individuals, societies and nations from decay and destruction—provides proof of the perfection of his guidance. It demonstrates that such a coherent, effective law could not have been originated by a man.

The greatest proof of his prophethood however, is the Qurʾān, a recital of the spoken words of Allāh. The Qurʾān was received and transmitted orally and is memorised by millions across the world. It is a lasting miracle characterised by inimitability (iʿjāz) and stands as an ongoing challenge for all of jinn and men combined to produce its like in eloquence, measured rhythmic beauty, depth of meaning, upright guidance, profound effect upon hearts and souls and many other affairs.

Muḥammad (ﷺ) was mentioned by name in the previous scriptures (in the languages of Hebrew and Aramaic) as מחמד "Muḥammad" (praised) and אחמד "Ahmad" (most praised). But those given scripture concealed this despite having full knowledge of it. Allāh (عَزَّوَجَلَّ) said regarding them:

الَّذِينَ آتَيْنَاهُمُ الْكِتَابَ يَعْرِفُونَهُ كَمَا يَعْرِفُونَ أَبْنَاءَهُمْ وَإِنَّ فَرِيقًا مِّنْهُمْ لَيَكْتُمُونَ الْحَقَّ وَهُمْ يَعْلَمُونَ

**"Those to whom We gave the Scripture know him as they know their own sons. But indeed, a party of them conceal the truth while they know [it]."** (2:146).

The learned from the People of the Book knew he was the "praised one" named and described in their scriptures. A prophet from the illiterate, from the offspring of **Kedar** (son of Ishmael) who would appear from the deserts of **Paran** in **a dry, arid place** (Hijāz, Mecca), glorifying Allāh. He would be the **chosen one** and **beloved** of Allāh, sent to **a nation of idol-worshippers.** He would be expelled from his city and be received near **Mount Sela** (Madīnah) by a people who would rejoice at his arrival. Later, with a large group of his followers, he would return to his city, **victorious over the idolators**. His **praise and mention** would be great and he would be given **a new recital or hymn** and come with **a law**. But a group of them rejected him, out of pride and arrogance, though they were convinced. Their scripture obligated them to believe in him and aid him because he brought that which confirmed the truth in previous scriptures.

**3. Requirements of this testification.** This testification for the messengership of Muḥammad (صَلَّىٰ ٱللَّٰهُ عَلَيْهِ وَسَلَّمَ) is an acknowledgement of rights that belong to the Messenger. They include the following:

a) To believe that Muḥammad (صَلَّىٰ ٱللَّٰهُ عَلَيْهِ وَسَلَّمَ) was the last and final prophet and messenger sent to all of jinn and men. That he was truthful in whatever he conveyed from his Lord with respect to the affairs of the seen and unseen, the past, present and the future. These affairs include knowledge regarding the Day of Judgement, Paradise, Hellfire, the stories of the prophets and the nations of the past. Likewise to believe he was truthful in all that he conveyed of commands, prohibitions and legislations:

فَآمِنُوا بِاللَّهِ وَرَسُولِهِ وَالنُّورِ الَّذِي أَنزَلْنَا

**"So believe in Allāh and His Messenger and in the light [of guidance] which we have revealed [to him]."** (64:8).

b) To worship Allāh only through the guidance of the Prophet. To obey him in whatever he commanded and prohibited and to take caution against his disobedience as it entails disobedience to Allāh (عَزَّوَجَلَّ). To limit oneself to his guidance and to his way (sunnah) and to not go beyond that. To refer differences and matters of dispute back to him and to the guidance he came with:

وَمَا آتَاكُمُ الرَّسُولُ فَخُذُوهُ وَمَا نَهَاكُمْ عَنْهُ فَانتَهُوا

**"Whatever the Messenger commands you, take it [and abide by it] and whatever he prohibits you from, refrain from it."** (59:7).

And the Prophet (صَلَّىٰ ٱللَّٰهُ عَلَيْهِ وَسَلَّمَ) said: "*Whoever obeys me has obeyed Allāh and whoever disobeys me has disobeyed Allāh.*"[23]

---

[23] Related by al-Bukhārī.

c) To respect and venerate him (tawqīr, taʿzīr) with what is due to him in accordance with his status. This entails honouring him and speaking about him within the limits of respect. It means to support him and to shield him from abuse and harm.

فَالَّذِينَ آمَنُوا بِهِ وَعَزَّرُوهُ وَنَصَرُوهُ وَاتَّبَعُوا النُّورَ الَّذِي أُنزِلَ مَعَهُ أُولَٰئِكَ هُمُ الْمُفْلِحُونَ

**"So those who believe in him, honour him, help him, and follow the light (the Qurʾān) which has been sent down with him, it is they who will be successful."** (7:157).

d) To love him more than anything else. The Prophet (ﷺ) said, "*None of you truly believes until I am more beloved to him than his own father, his son and all of mankind.*"[24] This is because he is a mercy to humankind and the benefit he brought—in terms of guidance in this world and deliverance in the hereafter—is far greater than all other joys and benefits a person may attain from any other person, be they parents, spouses, children, relatives, kings or leaders. Love of the Prophet (ﷺ) is a matter of the heart and its evidences are displayed outwardly in a person's actions. However, this love is not an exaggerated love such as what the Christians have done with Jesus (عَلَيْهِ السَّلَامُ) until they deified him. Likewise, what many have done with the saints or righteous people, exaggerating in them and turning them into idols that are worshipped alongside Allāh.

e) In connection with the previous point: From his rights is that his true status—a humble slave and messenger—is maintained and never exceeded either to the extreme of exaggeration (ghuluww) or to the extreme of neglect and belittlement (taqṣīr). He is the best of all humankind, the most superior of all the Prophets and Messengers, but alongside that he is also a human who does not know the unseen and does not have independent control over harm and benefit. Hence, he was commanded by Allāh to say:

قُل لَّا أَمْلِكُ لِنَفْسِي نَفْعًا وَلَا ضَرًّا إِلَّا مَا شَاءَ اللَّهُ وَلَوْ كُنتُ أَعْلَمُ الْغَيْبَ لَاسْتَكْثَرْتُ مِنَ الْخَيْرِ وَمَا مَسَّنِيَ السُّوءُ إِنْ أَنَا إِلَّا نَذِيرٌ وَبَشِيرٌ لِّقَوْمٍ يُؤْمِنُونَ

[24] Related by al-Bukhārī and Muslim.

**"Say [O Muḥammad]: 'I possess no power of benefit or hurt to myself except as Allāh wills. If I had the knowledge of the unseen, I should have secured for myself an abundance of wealth, and no evil should have touched me. I am but a warner, and a bringer of glad tidings to people who believe'."** (7:188).

A Muslim is prohibited from exaggerating in the status of the prophets and righteous as this is the starting point of paths which eventually lead to the greatest crime and injustice, **associationism** (shirk). The Prophet (صَلَّىٰ ٱللَّهُ عَلَيْهِ وَسَلَّمَ) placed barriers in front of all avenues which lead to excessive praise, exaggeration and eventual worship of people alongside Allāh, and this is another aspect of the perfection of his guidance.

f) Also from the rights of the Prophet (صَلَّىٰ ٱللَّهُ عَلَيْهِ وَسَلَّمَ) is to love his companions, his wives and the people of his household. To revile and belittle them is to harm the Prophet (صَلَّىٰ ٱللَّهُ عَلَيْهِ وَسَلَّمَ). They are mentioned only with goodness. Malice is not harboured towards them and forgiveness is sought for them. To speak ill of them as a whole, or the majority of them and accuse them of misguidance or disbelief, is hypocrisy and disbelief itself. The great Muslim scholar, Imām Aḥmad bin Ḥanbal (d. 855) said: "When you see a man mentioning the Companions of Allāh's Messenger (صَلَّىٰ ٱللَّهُ عَلَيْهِ وَسَلَّمَ) with evil, suspect his Islām."[25] There are those who ascribe to Islām whilst hating and reviling the Prophet's wives and companions, ascribing disbelief to them. In reality, they are the disbelievers and their association with Islām is one of hypocrisy, not sincerity.[26] It is impossible for a genuine believer in Moses (عَلَيْهِ ٱلسَّلَامُ) to revile those closest to Moses and for a genuine believer in Jesus (عَلَيْهِ ٱلسَّلَامُ) to revile those closest to Jesus. Likewise, it is impossible for a genuine believer in Muḥammad (صَلَّىٰ ٱللَّهُ عَلَيْهِ وَسَلَّمَ) to revile those closest to him.

In conclusion of this chapter, a Muslim respect and fulfil the rights of the Messenger (صَلَّىٰ ٱللَّهُ عَلَيْهِ وَسَلَّمَ) because there is no other way to fulfil the rights of Allāh (عَزَّوَجَلَّ) except by fulfilling them.

---

[25] Refer to *al-Bidāyah wal-Nihāyah* of Ibn Kathīr, 8/142.

[26] They are known as the Rāfiḍah, or the Shīʿah, they have enmity towards the wives and companions of the Prophet (صَلَّىٰ ٱللَّهُ عَلَيْهِ وَسَلَّمَ).

## The Conditions of the Declaration

Now that the meaning of the two testifications has been explained and made clear, it is vital to understand that this declaration—the word (kalimah) of Islām by which a person enters Islām—has certain conditions without which it is invalid.

The Muslim scholar, Wahb bin Munabbih (d. 732) said, when asked, "Is not '*Lā ilāha illallāh*' a key to Paradise?" He replied: "Yes, but there is no key except that it has teeth. If you brought a key that has teeth, it will be opened for you, otherwise it will not be opened for you."[27]

These conditions are derived from the texts of the Qur'ān and the Prophetic traditions by the scholars of Islām and Tawḥīd and they are seven in number:

1. **knowledge** ('ilm)
2. **certainty** (yaqīn)
3. **acceptance** (qabūl)
4. **compliance** (inqiyād)
5. **truthfulness** (ṣidq)
6. **sincerity** (ikhlāṣ)
7. **love** (maḥabbah)

A brief explanation of each condition is provided below.

**1. Knowledge ('ilm).** Mere utterance of the declaration of Islām is not sufficient. Rather, a person must have knowledge and understanding of what he or she is expressing such that it cancels out ignorance. A concise explanation of the meaning of the statement, "*Lā ilāha illallāh muḥammad rasūlullāh*" has preceded and comprises the minimal amount of knowledge and understanding a person must possess regarding it. Allāh (عَزَّوَجَلَّ) said:

فَاعْلَمْ أَنَّهُ لَا إِلَٰهَ إِلَّا اللَّهُ

**"Have knowledge therefore, that there is none worthy of worship but Allāh [alone]."** (47:19).

**2. Certainty (yaqīn).** This is a perfection of the first condition of knowledge. A person must have certainty in what he or she is declaring and be free of doubt, hesitation and wavering. It means to be certain of the truth that there is no deity worthy of being

---

[27] Related by al-Bukhārī in Kitāb al-Janā'iz.

worshipped except Allāh and of the futility of worshipping other deities besides Him. A person may fully grasp something, but may remain doubtful about its truth and not believe in it despite grasping it. Many people understand the notion of *pure monotheism (tawḥīd) in belief, speech and deed* very well, but that does not mean they are certain of its truth. Hence, possessing certainty negates doubt and is additional to having mere knowledge of the meaning of the statement. Allāh (عَزَّوَجَلَّ) said:

إِنَّمَا الْمُؤْمِنُونَ الَّذِينَ آمَنُوا بِاللَّهِ وَرَسُولِهِ ثُمَّ لَمْ يَرْتَابُوا

**"The believers are only the ones who have believed in Allāh and His Messenger and then doubt not."** (49:15)

**3. Acceptance (qabūl).** A person may grasp the meaning of the declaration of Islām, and may also be certain and convinced that it is the truth. However, these two conditions would not be sufficient until a person also accepts the requirements of this declaration. It is possible for a person to fully understand the meaning and also be certain about its truth, but out of arrogance and pride, refuse to accept it. Allāh (عَزَّوَجَلَّ) said of such people:

إِنَّهُمْ كَانُوا إِذَا قِيلَ لَهُمْ لَا إِلَٰهَ إِلَّا اللَّهُ يَسْتَكْبِرُونَ

**"Truly, when it was said to them: 'Lā ilāha illāllah' (none is worthy of worship but Allāh), they displayed arrogance."** (37:35).

Hence, acceptance is a necessary condition, it negates arrogance. It means to accept inwardly that one must respond to and abide by the necessities of this declaration, which are to worship Allāh alone and to do so through what He legislated and commanded by way of His Book and by way of the example of His Messenger (صَلَّى اللَّهُ عَلَيْهِ وَسَلَّمَ).

**4. Compliance (inqiyād).** Whilst acceptance is inward and is a person's acknowledgement that he or she is obligated to respond to and abide by the requirements of the declaration, compliance is outward and naturally follows from inward acceptance. By complying in one's beliefs, statements and deeds, a person is submitting to Allāh, the very meaning of Islām:

وَمَنْ أَحْسَنُ دِينًا مِّمَّنْ أَسْلَمَ وَجْهَهُ لِلَّهِ وَهُوَ مُحْسِنٌ وَاتَّبَعَ مِلَّةَ إِبْرَاهِيمَ حَنِيفًا

“**And who is better in religion than one who submits himself to Allāh while being a doer of good and follows the religion of Abraham, inclining toward truth?**” (4:125).

Together, inward acceptance and submission (qabūl, istislām) and outward compliance (inqiyād) symbolise the essence of Islām.

**5. Truthfulness (ṣidq).** This condition requires that a person is truthful in his or her declaration of Islām and truthful in his or her belief in its meaning. It opposes hypocrisy (nifāq).

There were people in the time of the Prophet (ﷺ) who expressed Islām outwardly whilst disbelieving inwardly. They either did not believe in the Qur'ān and the Prophet (ﷺ) or they were motivated to disbelieve inwardly whilst professing belief outwardly due to factors such as pride, hatred, jealousy and resentment or the desire to protect their worldly interests. Some of them also strove to extinguish the light of Islām through stealth and intrigue.

Since what is in the heart must manifest itself outwardly, there are recognisable traits of hypocrisy which cannot be reconciled with genuine faith. Truthfulness is when the inward and outward are in agreement. What is in the heart must agree with what is said by the tongue and performed by the limbs.

Allāh (عَزَّوَجَلَّ) said:

إِذَا جَاءَكَ الْمُنَافِقُونَ قَالُوا نَشْهَدُ إِنَّكَ لَرَسُولُ اللَّهِ وَاللَّهُ يَعْلَمُ إِنَّكَ لَرَسُولُهُ وَاللَّهُ يَشْهَدُ إِنَّ الْمُنَافِقِينَ لَكَاذِبُونَ

“**When the hypocrites come to you, [O Muḥammad], they say, ‘We testify that you are the Messenger of Allāh.’ And Allāh knows that you are His Messenger, and Allāh testifies that the hypocrites are liars.**” (63:1).

The Prophet (ﷺ) said: “*There is no person who testifies that none has the right to be worshipped but Allāh [alone] and that Muḥammad is the Messenger of Allāh, truthfully from his heart, except that Allāh makes Hellfire unlawful for him.*”[28]

Hence, truthfulness is from the most important of conditions.

---

[28] Related by al-Bukhārī in Kitāb al-ʿIlm.

**6. Sincerity (ikhlāṣ).** Sincerity is to make all of one's worship for Allāh alone. It is also to purify the heart from showing off and doing deeds to be seen and heard of by others. Allāh (عَزَّوَجَلَّ) said:

وَمَا أُمِرُوا إِلَّا لِيَعْبُدُوا اللَّهَ مُخْلِصِينَ لَهُ الدِّينَ حُنَفَاءَ

**"And they were not commanded except to worship Allāh , [being] sincere to Him in religion, inclining to truth."** (98:5).

Hence, sincerity is to perform deeds for the sake of Allāh alone and not for the pleasure, praise and acceptance of others. If actions are done for Allāh and also for the sake of other people, then they will be rejected. A sign of major hypocrisy—which entails disbelief—is when the *overwhelming majority* of a person's deeds are for show.

**7. Love (maḥabbah).** A person loves the truth which is the declaration that nothing has the right to be worshipped but Allāh alone. He or she also loves to abide by its requirements, and loves those who believe and act upon it. A sign of love is that a person follows and implements the guidance of the Messenger:

قُلْ إِن كُنتُمْ تُحِبُّونَ اللَّهَ فَاتَّبِعُونِي يُحْبِبْكُمُ اللَّهُ وَيَغْفِرْ لَكُمْ ذُنُوبَكُمْ وَاللَّهُ غَفُورٌ رَّحِيمٌ

**"Say [O Muḥammad]: 'If you (really) love Allāh then follow me, Allāh will love you and forgive you of your sins. And Allāh is Oft-Forgiving, Most Merciful'."** (3:31).

Any claim of inward love, devoid of outward following and compliance is an empty claim. It is like a husband claiming to love his wife or a father claiming to love his child, yet not a single outward expression of love—in speech or deed—has ever emanated from him. This is impossible. The claim that faith is only in the heart is false. Rather, faith is belief, speech and deed, and all of this must be in agreement with authentic Prophetic guidance.

In summary, these are the seven conditions of the declaration of Islām which a Muslim must learn, know, understand and apply because they entail preservation of true, sound, acceptable religion. They provide a Muslim with a key that has "teeth" enabling him or her to open the door to Paradise.

## The Nature and Reality of Worship

The essence of Islam is comprised within these two testifications and they indicate two foundational elements of sound religion:

**First:** That Allāh is exclusively worshipped alone, no partners are associated with Him in worship. As for the types of worship, they are many and include, by way of example: love (maḥabbah), fear (khawf), hope (rajāʾ), reliance (tawakkul), bowing (sujūd), prostration (rukūʿ), prayer (ṣālāt), invocation (duʿā), seeking aid (istiʿānah), soliciting rescue (istighāthah). Worship is inward, in the heart, consisting of its belief and its feelings, emotions and states. And it is also outward, on the tongue and limbs, consisting of utterances and deeds. True, lasting satisfaction and serenity only settle and remain in the heart through the worship and remembrance of Allāh.

**Second:** That He is not worshipped except through what He legislated. Acts of worship follow the principles of legislation (sharʿ) and imitation (ittibāʿ) of the Messenger of Allāh (صَلَّىٰٱللَّهُعَلَيۡهِوَسَلَّمَ) in what he conveyed of the law. It is not for anyone to worship Allāh except through what His Messenger legislated of the obligatory and recommended deeds. He is not worshipped through innovated statements and actions for which He gave no authority, as this leads to alteration and distortion of true religion. This is what the Jews and Christians fell into when they innovated into their religion. Thus every act of worship must be founded upon pure monotheistic belief, directed only to Allāh, done sincerely for His sake and be in agreement with the Prophetic guidance regarding its details, general and specific.

The message of the Prophets combines between these two foundations with the second being a means for the fulfilment of the first.[29] Islām—to worship Allāh alone and to worship Him only through what He legislated and ordered—is the way of Abraham, Isaac, Ishmael, Jacob, Moses, David, Solomon, the Israelite prophets, Jesus and Muḥammad (صَلَّىٰٱللَّهُعَلَيۡهِوَسَلَّمَ).

---

[29] In Islām, whilst deeds are essential to faith and are required for salvation, they are not the sole, independent cause. None will enter Paradise except through the grace, mercy and forgiveness of Allāh.

## True and False Religion

From what has preceded, we should know that correct religion is to worship Allāh alone through obedience to His Messengers in what they legislated. Corrupt religion is to worship other than Allāh, which is **associationism** (shirk) or to worship Allāh through acts of worship having no basis in revelation which is **innovation** (bidʿah).

Further, sound religion combines between beneficial knowledge and righteous action. Knowledge without deeds earns wrath. Deeds performed upon ignorance, in absence of knowledge, is misguidance. Salvation [after the grace and mercy of Allāh] is through beneficial knowledge and righteous action combined and this is because of the necessary and inseparable connection between the heart and the body. What is in the heart of knowledge, conviction and submission must manifest outwardly on the limbs and what is performed by the limbs in turn must have a necessary impact upon what is in heart. Thus, the states of love, fear, hope, reliance and others in the heart must manifest outwardly, as righteous deeds. And outward deeds such as remembrance, prayer, seeking forgiveness, repentance, charity, prayer in turn have a real, tangible effect upon the heart. It is impossible for faith to settle in the heart without outward manifestation on the tongue and limbs unless there are preventive barriers in the heart which constitute disbelief such as arrogance (kibr) or hypocrisy (nifāq).

Whoever believes that by merely uttering the two testifications alone a person will enter Paradise and never enter Hellfire at all has opposed the Book, the Prophetic tradition and consensus. Rather, a person only deserves entry into Paradise and deliverance from Hellfire through inward belief and acceptance *coupled with* outward expression, observance and compliance.

This leads us to reframe the two testifications into a number of criteria that separate between true and false religion. They can be formulated in the form of the following questions:

a) Who or what do you worship?
b) How do you worship?
c) How do you attain salvation and Paradise?
d) What is the source of your religion?

Through these questions we are able evaluate all religions. Thus true religion, Islām, is that you worship none but Allāh alone; that you worship Him only through what He legislated; that you attain Paradise through righteous deeds [though Allāh's grace and mercy are the ultimate cause of salvation]; and that your source of guidance is uncorrupted revelation from Allāh (عَزَّوَجَلَّ).

Anything besides true, authentic religion will fail one or more of these criteria through the following:

a) Denial of a creator to begin with such as what is found in the religions of **Atheism**, **Materialism** and **Philosophical Naturalism**. These are conjectural, speculative, pessimistic belief systems concealed behind the veil of science to give them a cloak of authenticity and authority.[30] They are cleverly defined as "*absence* of belief in a creator" so as to avoid the burden of proof being applied to them. They are more accurately defined as "*belief* in the absence of a creator". This is of course pure conjecture for which they have no proof. In order to explain creation, they ascribe divine qualities to nature and matter in a cryptic manner, through complex, technical language. The speculative beliefs of the atheists and materialists are simply the imaginations of their minds made to appear real and true through theoretical physics and clever mathematics, not empirical science. The only difference between them and the primitives is that the primitives worshipped nature after giving it divine qualities, whereas these moderns give nature divine qualities to explain away the Creator so as to escape from having to worship Him, out of pride and arrogance. The primitives were more coherent than the arrogant moderns from one angle and the moderns are shrewder than the primitives from another angle.

b) Erecting and worshipping other deities such as what is found in **Hinduism**, a pantheistic[31] or panentheistic[32] belief system, or

[30] Scientific knowledge in the fields of cosmic annd biological origins is admittedly speculative and conjectural, not empirical or factual.

[31] The belief that all of reality is equal to God, that everything which exists is a divine manifestation and there is no such thing as God and "His creation". Concisely, *all is God.*

[32] The belief that the universe is contained within God who enters and interpenetrates it. Concisely, *all is within God.*

**Christianity** in which Jesus (عَلَيْهِ السَّلَامُ) is made divine and worshipped alongside Allāh. Some sects like the Catholics also worship Mary (عَلَيْهَا السَّلَامُ), the mother of Jesus, as well as saints. Monotheism is not simply the belief in only one, supreme creator since the majority of the inhabitants of the earth already acknowledge this through innate disposition. Rather, monotheism is to single out this creator alone with all forms and types of worship. This was the call of Noah, Abraham, Moses, Jesus and Muḥammad (صَلَّى اللَّهُ عَلَيْهِ وَسَلَّمَ) and all prophets. Other polytheistic religions include **Kemetism**, a modern revival of ancient Egyptian paganism and worship of Thoth, Ma'at and Rā (the sun god). Likewise, **Shintoism**, a Japanese ethnic religion in which spirits, essences and gods are worshipped.

c) **Buddhism** denies an inherent purpose for life and as such does not teach belief in gods, asserting they are cultural in origin but may be used as part of one's spiritual development. Hence it is atheistic in principle but allows incorporation of gods for the attainment of its primary goal: to remove suffering by escaping the continuous cycle of death and rebirth through ethical precepts in order to reach the state of "nirvana" (liberation). Any system of spirituality that is not based on a Creator and pure monotheism is false and defective.

d) Claiming that superiority or salvation is based around tribe and race such as what is found within **Judaism** of the concept of "the chosen people" or with the black nationalist supremacists such as the **Nation of Islām** (a spurious title)[33] or the **Black Hebrew Israelites** whose teachings revolve around resentment, anger and hatred on the basis of race and events of history.

e) A distorted, corrupted, altered scripture such as what is found with the **Jews** and **Christians** who altered the Torah and Gospel respectively and worship through other than what Allāh revealed and legislated. In **Rabbinic Judaism**, the Rabbis assume divine character and authority, claiming that Allāh continues to speak and reveal to the Jews through them. The Jews and Christians innovated

---

[33] The Nation of Islām are not Muslims but imposters using the name of Islām to conceal their heretical and idolatrous beliefs. They believe that God was incarnated in the form of Elijah Muhammad (d. 1975), that black people are divine whilst white men are devils. They have many beliefs that clash with the revealed books and the teachings of the prophets and messengers.

into their religion, distorted their scripture, worshipped Allāh with beliefs and actions for which He gave no authority and abandoned much of what they were commanded with.

f) The absence of revelation and prophethood—the sources of authentic, true religion—such as what is found with **Sikhism** which is a philosophical system devised by men by combining what they borrowed from other religions. It is not free of pantheistic or panentheistic elements influenced by Hinduism with a confusing incoherent, contradictory, speculative theology. If it had been true religion based on genuine, uncorrupted revelation, such incoherence in its basic teachings about the Creator would not be found.

The above are merely illustrations and the reader should be able to apply the aforementioned criteria in a like manner to evaluate any religion of choice.

In conclusion, Islām is the name of *true religion*. Allāh (عَزَّوَجَلَّ) said:

أَفَغَيْرَ دِينِ اللَّهِ يَبْغُونَ وَلَهُ أَسْلَمَ مَن فِي السَّمَاوَاتِ وَالْأَرْضِ طَوْعًا وَكَرْهًا وَإِلَيْهِ يُرْجَعُونَ

**"Do they seek other than [Islām], the religion of Allāh, while to Him submit all creatures in the Heavens and the Earth, willingly or unwillingly, and to Him shall they all be returned?"** (3:83).

This is known through its meaning which is submitting to the will of the Creator [guided by authentic revealed knowledge that enjoins beneficial righteous action]. Islām is a state of being and hence, is not defined by or restricted to a location, race, tribe or individual.

Judaism and Christianity are not the names by which Moses and Jesus (عَلَيْهِمَاالسَّلَامُ) referred to their teachings. Judaism is based on tribalism and the name of "Christianity" which is Greek in origin is based around the person of Jesus. Hinduism is named after a geographic region. Buddhism is named after its founder, Siddartha Gautama, whilst Sikhism has a strong ethnic character to it.

The names of religions besides Islām generally follow this pattern. All the Prophets and Messengers called to Islām and they were *Muslims*, those who submit to the will of Allāh and serve Him. The religion acceptable to Allāh has no other name but *Islām*.

## The Remaining Four Pillars of Islām

By uttering the two testifications a person has established the first and greatest pillar and is thereby required to establish the remaining four pillars. We shall discuss them briefly here from the angle of their goals, benefits and virtues rather than their practical details which can be learned separately.

**Purification (ṭahārah) and the five daily prayers (ṣalāḥ).** Just as worship is invalid in the absence of monotheism (tawḥīd), prayer is invalid in the absence of physical purity. Islām is founded upon purity, whether doctrinal, spiritual or physical. Purification is one half of faith and is the key to prayer just as pure monotheism is the foundation of Islām and the key to worship.

The prayer is obligatory upon every male and female who has reached the age of maturity. It is performed at set times in a state of physical purity through ablution (wuḍū') wherein the hands, face, arms and feet are washed. The prayer consists of actions, statements and feelings and include standing, bowing, prostrating, supplicating, remembering, sincerity, love, hope, humility, awe and other affairs which make it the greatest pillar after the two testifications. It is of tremendous impact upon the heart, soul and body and restrains from improper conduct.

Allāḥ (عَزَّوَجَلَّ) said:

إِنَّ الصَّلَاةَ تَنْهَىٰ عَنِ الْفَحْشَاءِ وَالْمُنكَرِ

**"Indeed [establishing] the prayer prevents from immorality and wrongdoing."** (29:45)

Every limb and organ is a recipient of the favours and blessings of Allāh. The prayer involves the entire body with all the major limbs of the body engaged in worship and gratitude. The prayer washes away sins, purifies the heart and soul, brings one closer to his or her Lord and provides serenity and satisfaction to the heart.

**Fasting (ṣawm).** Fasting is to withhold from food, drink, sexual relations and all unlawful deeds between dawn and sunset for thirty days during the month of Ramaḍān. It is a month of tremendous mercy and blessing in which a Muslim increases in remembrance, prayer and charity. It leads a person to increase in piety.

يَا أَيُّهَا الَّذِينَ آمَنُوا كُتِبَ عَلَيْكُمُ الصِّيَامُ كَمَا كُتِبَ عَلَى الَّذِينَ مِن قَبْلِكُمْ لَعَلَّكُمْ تَتَّقُونَ

**"O you who have believed, decreed upon you is fasting as it was decreed upon those before you that you may become pious."** (2:183).

Fasting comprises many tremendous benefits and wisdoms. It helps one to develop sympathy for the poor and needy of the world and in turn, to become more appreciative and grateful for the favours and bounties of Allāh. It leads a person to become more patient and disciplined. Numerous health benefits of fasting are often mentioned by some, but they are only secondary in nature and are not the primary reason for the legislation of fasting.

**Obligatory charity (zakāh).** A Muslim who has wealth stored and unused for a year that reaches a certain threshold value must give a small amount of it—one fortieth (2.5%)—in obligatory charity. It is payable only on certain types of wealth such as gold, silver, cash, agricultural products, livestock and trade inventories. Zakāh purifies one's wealth, instils generosity and kindness, makes one detached from wealth with the realisation that all wealth is the property of Allāh, is only of temporary possession and will not be taken to the grave. The society benefits through redistribution of wealth from where it is not needed to where it is needed most, leading to a stimulation in the economy through constant movement of wealth. This is achieved without impoverishing the wealthy.

**Pilgrimage (Ḥajj).** The final pillar is the pilgrimage to Mecca which is obligatory for those who have the financial means to perform it. A series of rituals are performed at a specific time during the last month of the Islāmic calendar, Dhul-Ḥijjah, at specified locations. They are a reminder of the series of trials faced by Abraham (عَلَيْهِ السَّلَامُ), the pure, upright monotheist. The pilgrimage is replete with lessons in monotheism, purification of the soul, patience, sacrifice, racial equality and harmony, unity and much more.

## The Six Pillars of Īmān (Faith)

We have completed our discussion of Islām. **Islām is outward.** All of its pillars are statements and deeds which are heard and observed by others. Inward belief, truthfulness, sincerity and acceptance of the heart validate outward Islām. Their absence would turn any outward display of Islām into hypocrisy.

Hence, a **minimal threshhold** of inward belief is required to validate the outward Islām, and the heart is the seat of that belief. This minimal threshhold of inward belief relates to the two testifications as has preceded and then around six pillars of belief. There is a generalised belief which a Muslim must have with respect to each of these pillars. These six pillars relate to what is *unseen*. Meaning, what cannot be experienced with the senses in the life of this world. Believing in the unseen is the first quality of the believer mentioned in the Qurʾān. Believing in the unseen is rational and warranted. There is no person on earth but must believe in what cannot been seen or perceived, either because they are not present to see it or because it cannot be seen due to limitations in vision.[34]

Allāh cannot be seen in this life though He can be known in a limited way through the effects and traces of His actions of creating and regulating. Allāh reveals more detailed knowledge of Himself through revelation. Beings which Allāh created and are outside the realm of human perception, such as angels and jinn, also cannot be seen. The previous revealed books and sent messengers are from the unseen for us as we were not present to witness them. The Last Day, the Day of Judgement, is a matter of the unseen. The Divine Decree, that Allāh created His creation through natural laws, through cause-effect mechanism, gave everything its due form, its properties and

---

[34] Scientists believe in the unseen and invent things such as "black holes" and numerous forces and particles which are hypothetical and undetectable. Though they cannot see these things because of physical impossibility, they nevertheless try to detect them indirectly, by tracing their effects. Atheists like Richard Dawkins speak of the plausibility of aliens from other worlds as a means of explaining life on earth. This also implies belief in the unseen. Evolutionists whose doctrine is built upon the claim that a self-replicating cell arose through pure random interactions also believe in the unseen. No one can escape from believing in at least something from the unseen.

precise measure and has all-encompassing, perfect knowledge of what occurred, is occurring and is yet to occur, is also a matter of the unseen requiring faith. The six pillars are mentioned in the following two verses, first the statement of Allāh (عَزَّوَجَلَّ):

وَلَٰكِنَّ الْبِرَّ مَنْ آمَنَ بِاللَّهِ وَالْيَوْمِ الْآخِرِ وَالْمَلَائِكَةِ وَالْكِتَابِ وَالنَّبِيِّينَ

**"But righteousness is [the quality of] the one who believes in Allāh, the Last Day, the Angels, the Books and the Prophets."** (2:177).

And also:

إِنَّا كُلَّ شَيْءٍ خَلَقْنَاهُ بِقَدَرٍ

**"Indeed, all things have we created with predetermined, due measure."** (54:49).

We will briefly outline the minimal amount of faith a person must have for each of these six pillars.

**1. Belief in Allāh.** A discussion of belief in Allāh has preceded in the explanation of the two testifications. We can summarise the essential elements here. Belief in Allāh is to have faith in His absolute oneness and uniqueness. He is **unique in His lordship** (al-rubūbiyyah), **unique in His names and attributes** (al-asmāʾ wal-ṣifāt) and on the basis of these two, **unique in His right to worship** (ulūhiyyah). Thus, Allāh is one and unique in His dominion and His actions of creating, owning, regulating and providing, **having no partner** (sharīk) therein. He is unique in His names and attributes, **having no equal** (naẓīr) therein. And He is one and unique in His right to be worshipped, **having no rival** (nidd) therein. Thus, a Muslim believes that Allāh is singled out with all forms and types of worship including love, fear, hope, reliance, supplication, bowing, prostrating and so on.

**2. Belief in the Angels.** To have firm belief that the angels are a creation from Allāh's creations and are honourable servants.

They have bodies made of imperceptible light and are able to take on forms and appearances. They possess great strength and also have the ability to travel at great velocities. By their nature, they worship Allāh, only ever obey Him and never disobey Him. They have reason and understanding and have the qualities of knowledge, nobility and humility amongst others. They inhabit the heavens and never tire of worship. They do not have independent power to create or regulate but they are entrusted with tasks and duties in Allāh's creation. Some angels, such as Gabriel (Jibrīl), are entrusted with revelation. Others, such as Michael (Mīkāʾīl), with rain and plants, vegetation. Another angel, Isrāfīl, is tasked with blowing the horn to signal the arrival of the Last Day. Others are tasked with taking souls at death. Others with the mountains or what is in the wombs. Others are scribes that record and others are keepers of Paradise and Hellfire. From having faith in the angels is to love them and have loyalty to them. Through them, Allāh operates His creation and they symbolise His power, majesty and grandeur. It is unlawful to worship them or to channel worship through them. They are no more than humble servants.

**3. Belief in Revealed Books.** To have firm belief in the various books that Allāh revealed to His messengers. These books comprise His speech and convey truth, light and guidance. The revealed books establish **the uncreated attribute of speech** (kalām) for Allāh. Since His essence is uncreated, then all of His attributes are uncreated, as are His actions.

The revealed books include the **Scrolls** (Ṣuḥuf) of Abraham, the **Torah** (Tawrāt) given to Moses, the **Psalms** (Zābūr) given to David, the **Gospel** (Injīl) given to Jesus and the **Recital** (Qurʾān) given to Muḥammad (ﷺ). The foundation of all revealed books and divine legislation are the Torah and the Qurʾān,. The Psalms of David were a prelude for the Gospel (Injīl) and the Gospel was a prelude for the Qurʾān.

The previous books underwent alteration, addition, deletion and distortion, whilst others were lost. All previous books are abrogated by the Qurʾān which corroborates and affirms whatever truth they contain in their present form. Hence, a Muslim has a generalised belief in the original revelations of these books. He does not affirm anything in the current versions of what are claimed to be the revelations given to Moses and Jesus (عَلَيْهِمَا ٱلسَّلَامُ) unless it agrees with the Qurʾān and the Prophetic traditions. As for whatever is besides this, a Muslim neither rejects nor affirms it.

The Qurʾān is a recital and is not primarily a written text. It was memorised by thousands and then transmitted orally (as well as in secondary written form) through each generation till today where millions of Muslims have the entire text memorised. If every printed or electronic copy of the Qur'ān was erased instantly, the Muslims, through collaboration, would have it rewritten from memory within the hour. This is just one of the numerous aspects of its unique, miraculous, inimitable nature. The Qur'ān is guidance, mercy and light and guides to that which is upright.

**4. Belief in the Messengers.** To have firm belief that messengers have been sent to every nation inviting them to worship Allāh alone and reject false deities. To believe they were upon truth and guidance and were given signs and evidences to establish their truthfulness and the truth of the message they were sent with. To believe that they conveyed their message as entrusted and were aided and supported by Allāh against their unjust enemies. Some of these messengers have been named and others have not. Hence, one must believe in all of them with a generalised belief without separating or distinguishing between them in principle.

From the greatest of these messengers are the five resolute messengers, so described in the Qur'ān, and they are **Noah**, **Abraham**, **Moses**, **Jesus** (عَلَيْهِمُ السَّلَامُ) and **Muḥammad** (صَلَّىٰ اللَّهُ عَلَيْهِ وَسَلَّمَ). They possessed tremendous resolve, patience and diligence and were greatly tested. The previous prophets named in the Qur'ān are:

1. Adam
2. Idrīs
3. Noah
4. Hūd
5. Ṣāliḥ
6. Lot
7. Abraham
8. Ishmael
9. Isaac
10. Jacob
11. Joseph
12. Shu'ayb
13. Aaron
14. Moses
15. David
16. Solomon
17. Job
18. Ezekiel
19. Jonah
20. Elias
21. Elisha
22. Zechariah
23. John
24. Jesus

All of the Prophets and Messengers were created men. They were not divine, did not claim to be and never called to their own worship. Like all other humans, they ate food, drank water and were subject to illnesses. Allāh favoured them with prophethood or messengership and aided them with miracles. They were upright, noble men who were not known to commit major sins.[35] There are three categories amongst them: Prophets, Prophet-kings and Slave-messengers. The Slave-messengers are the most superior. The most superior witin this category is Muḥammad (صَلَّى ٱللَّهُ عَلَيْهِ وَسَلَّمَ) and then the remaining four resolute messengers: Noah, Abraham, Moses and Jesus (عَلَيْهِمُ ٱلسَّلَامُ). While It is impermissible to distinguish between them in the *foundation* of prophethood—in regards to which they are equal—some of them nevertheless may excel over others in one aspect or more. The most complete and perfect of them is Muḥammad (صَلَّى ٱللَّهُ عَلَيْهِ وَسَلَّمَ), the Seal of the Prophets and Messengers.

A believer must show love and loyalty towards all of them, believe in their excellences and virtues, defend their honours from ridicule and mockery, and invoke peace, blessings and mercy upon them. To disbelieve in one of them is to disbelieve in all of them and to show enmity to one of them is to show enmity to all of them.

A unique aspect of Muḥammad's (صَلَّى ٱللَّهُ عَلَيْهِ وَسَلَّمَ) messengership is that he was sent to all jinn and men with the final revelation, the Qurʾān. His call was universal and was not restricted to his own people. Every claim to prophethood after Muḥammad (صَلَّى ٱللَّهُ عَلَيْهِ وَسَلَّمَ) is a futile claim whose futility is recognised easily, through simple analysis.[36]

**5. Belief in the Last Day**. To have firm belief in the Day of Judgement in which people will be resurrected, held to account for their deeds and recompensed, good with good and evil with evil, with complete and perfect justice being established and no one being wronged even an atom's weight. Belief in the Day of Judgement incorporates belief in other affairs such as the **minor** and **major signs** of the Day of Judgement, what happens in **the grave**, and the various events taking place on the Day of Judgement—such as the **gathering**, the **drinking pool**, the **scales**, the **bridge over Hellfire**, and **various intercessions**—until those destined for Paradise enter Paradise and those destined for Hellfire enter Hellfire.

---

[35] The Torah is replete with evil lies and fabrications against some of the Prophets that were inserted by the lying, oppressive pens of the scribes.

[36] The claim that there is another prophet after Muḥammad (صَلَّى ٱللَّهُ عَلَيْهِ وَسَلَّمَ)—such as the claim of the Aḥmadīs (Qādiyānīs) that Mirza Ghulām Aḥmad (d. 1908) was a prophet—constitutes pure, original disbelief (kufr).

Evidence for the plausibility of resurrection is all around us in the continuous, repeat cycles of birth, death and rebirth of living things. In the Qur'ān, Allāh (عَزَّوَجَلَّ) draws attention to these realities by giving similitudes for the resurrection to show that it is not far-fetched. The mechanism(s) through which it will occur are like the mechanisms of revival we routinely witness and experience around us:

وَاللَّهُ الَّذِي أَرْسَلَ الرِّيَاحَ فَتُثِيرُ سَحَابًا فَسُقْنَاهُ إِلَىٰ بَلَدٍ مَّيِّتٍ فَأَحْيَيْنَا بِهِ الْأَرْضَ بَعْدَ مَوْتِهَا كَذَٰلِكَ النُّشُورُ

"**And it is Allāh who sends the winds, and they stir and raise the clouds, and We drive them to a dead land and give life thereby to the earth after its lifelessness. Thus will be the resurrection.**" (35:9).

Reflection upon such phenomena are a reminder of the ease with which Allāh gives life to things after their death.

Belief in the Last Day bears numerous fruits, from them:

a) It makes a person become eager for righteousness and to aspire for Allāh's pleasure and reward.

b) It consoles a person in that whatever he misses out on in this life, he or she will receive that which is better, greater and more lasting in the next.

c) It allows a person to perceive and feel the justice of Allāh in that everyone will be recompensed in accordance with his or her actions and even if wrongdoers escape justice in this life, they will not escape it in the next.[37]

**6. Belief in the Divine Determination and Decree.** To have firm belief that Allāh has all-encompassing prior knowledge of all that is to occur in His creation. That all things (natural laws and cause-effect mechanisms) have been created with precise measure and nothing takes place except through His creation and command. That good and evil, life and death, health and sickness, belief and disbelief have been decreed to occur in accordance with His foreknowledge and

---

[37] Denial of resurrection—as is found with naturalists, materialists and atheists—leads to a dark, pessimistic, gloomy outlook in life and invites people to take as much advantage of this life as possible at the expense of the lives and welfare of others. Thus, the greatest mass murders in history took place at the hands of atheistic communists in the 20th century.

wisdom. That He is the doer of whatever He wills, whatever He wills occurs and whatever He does not will does not occur.

There are four levels to belief in divine determination and decree:

a) To believe in Allāh's **all-encompassing knowledge** (ʿilm) of all existing and non-existing things (whether possible or impossible) and the when and how of all that has taken place or is yet to take place, and of all that has not or will not take place but which if it had, when and how it would have taken place.

b) To believe that all of this knowledge has been **written** down in a register known as the Preserved Tablet (al-lawḥ al-maḥfūẓ).

c) To believe in Allāh's **all-inclusive will** (mashīʾah), such that whatever He wills occurs and whatever He does not will does not occur.

d) To believe in Allāh's **all-encompassing creative power** (khalq). He brings things into existence and makes things happen at the precise moment He wills them through His total control over matter, energy, forces, natural laws and all cause-effect mechanisms.

All of these levels are indicated in the Qurʾān.[38]

There is nothing in this which implies lack of choice and free will or injustice and this is known by a couple of simple analogies:

First, when a person has a choice to travel through and reside in a pleasant, peaceful town in which one's safety and welfare is guaranteed, he or she will make the informed, rational choice to travel through it as opposed to a town of crime, violence, theft and murder, when both options are readily available. Second, when any person is wronged by another in relation to his or her person or possessions, he or she demands justice—which implies that the one who committed the wrong was acting with free will. A wronged person never says, "Since the wrongdoer had no free will, I will not demand justice." Had this been the case, then the concept of justice would be non-existent, all laws would be void and all personal rights would be abolished. But no one ever thinks likes or acts upon the basis of such thoughts. As such, day to day human conduct falsifies such a claim.

---

[38] Refer to (65:12) for knowledge; (22:70), (36:12) for the record; (36:82), (81:29) for will; and (39:62), (37:96) for creative power.

Hence, free will is established for everyone. However, since Allāh created humans and gave them the faculties of hearing, seeing, feeling, reflecting, choosing, willing and doing, then He is **the creator** of their actions, whilst they are **the doers** of their actions. They do not and cannot escape the all-encompassing knowledge, all-inclusive will and all-encompassing creative power of Allāh. At the same time, they are never compelled in their actions. Allāh sent books and messengers to show them the path of safety and the path of harm, allowing them to freely and readily choose between guidance and misguidance, truth and falsehood.

Injustice would have been if Allāh had judged and then rewarded and punished purely on the basis of His prior knowledge alone, without His creatures having the ability and opportunity to choose and act. Hence, He created them, gave them the aforementioned faculties and sent them guidance, allowing them to freely choose without compulsion. They will be held accountable and rewarded or punished on the basis of their chosen actions, not on the basis of Allāh's prior knowledge alone. Hence, there is no injustice at all.

There were some amongst the Philosophers and astray Muslim sects who claimed that Allāh has no knowledge of events before they happen or that He only knows the universals, the general details (such as the general existence of men, trees and birds) but not the particulars, the specifics (such as a specific man, tree or bird, by name or type). This is disbelief (kufr) and invalidates Islām.

There were others who claimed that man is *the creator* of his own actions and that Allāh has no creative power or role in man's actions. This is tantamount to affirming two creators as is done by the Magian fire-worshippers who believe in a god of light and good and a god of darkness and evil. It is to put man outside the all-inclusive will and creative power of Allāh, which means that creators exist outside the domain of His will and power, beyond His control and subjugation. They invented this claim upon false reasoning, asserting that if man wills and acts within the domain of Allāh's will and creative power, then reward and punishment cannot be justified and also, that in such a case, *evil deeds* would be ascribed to Allāh.

The truth in this matter is that Allāh is **the creator** of man and his deeds, but not **the doer** of man's deeds. Allāh is the creator of all matter, energy, natural laws and cause-effect mechanisms through which man comes to be, exists, subsists, lives, thinks, reflects, speaks, chooses and acts. He cannot escape such laws and is bound by them. Hence, Allāh is **the creator** of man and his actions, good or bad, and man is merely the performer, **the doer** of his actions, not the creator. When a person gives charity, Allāh created that act because He created that person's body, its powers, abilities and its attributes. But it is the person who performed the act with his limbs. Likewise, when a person steals or murders someone, it was Allāh who created the act, but it was the person who physically performed the act, not Allāh:

وَاللَّهُ خَلَقَكُمْ وَمَا تَعْمَلُونَ

"**And Allāh created you and that which you [make or] do**." (37:96)

Allāh is the creator of all men's deeds and evil is not ascribed to Him because in relation to His acts of creating there are wisdoms.[39] Evil only emanates and resides within His creation. Thus, it is said about the deeds of men, "evil". But in relation to Allāh's actions of allowing evil deeds to take place, it is said "for a wisdom". Such wisdoms are sometimes mentioned in the revealed texts:

ظَهَرَ ٱلْفَسَادُ فِى ٱلْبَرِّ وَٱلْبَحْرِ بِمَا كَسَبَتْ أَيْدِى ٱلنَّاسِ لِيُذِيقَهُم بَعْضَ ٱلَّذِى عَمِلُوا۟ لَعَلَّهُمْ يَرْجِعُونَ

"**Evil has appeared on the land and sea because of what the hands of people have earned so that He may let them taste part of [the consequence of] what they have done that perhaps they will return [to righteousness]**." (30:41).

[39] Everything that we see to be "evil" in this world—such as oppression, death, disease and calamities—is evil in relation to us, but in terms of Allāh's actions of creating and allowing it, there are wisdoms. Thus, by death, life is appreciated; by poverty, prosperity is appreciated; by sickness, health is appreciated; by injustice, justice is appreciated; by evil, good is appreciated. Everything takes on meaning and purpose due to these contrasting affairs, and truth and justice arise through them. This is all from the wisdom of Allāh. Evil is not ascribed to Him at all. When a surgeon performs on a patient (who chose an unhealthy lifestyle and fell ill) and inflicts pain in the process, then in relation to the patient it is painful and evil, but in relation to the surgeon, his act is an act of wisdom and benefit.

Sometimes the wisdoms may be known to us in a general or specific sense and sometimes hidden from or obscure to us. Thus, in Allāh's actions there are far-reaching wisdoms which may not always be knowable, and hence, the statement of Allāh (عَزَّوَجَلَّ):

لَا يُسْأَلُ عَمَّا يَفْعَلُ وَهُمْ يُسْأَلُونَ

"**He is not questioned about what He does, but they will be questioned.**" (21:23).

There are many fruits of belief in divine determination and decree and they include:

a) Encouragement to depend upon Allāh (tawakkul) by adopting the ways and means since He is the Creator of all natural laws and cause-effect mechanisms. It encourages a person to strive for both the worldly affairs and those of the hereafter. It is foolish for a person to say that if Allāh has decreed for his hunger to be removed, then there is no need for him to eat, just as it is foolish for a person to say that if Allāh has decreed Paradise for him, there is no need for him to act, since all things are through ways and means, causes and effects.

b) Peace, serenity and calmness for the heart and soul because a person knows that all things are by Allāh's decree and that whatever afflicted him was never going to miss him and whatever missed him was never going to come to him. This helps to inculcate patience by which a person sees through hardships, difficulties and calamities and repels anxiety, stress and grief with ease.

c) Humility and not being amazed with oneself since all things attained by any person are favours bestowed by Allāh. A person only acquires things through the ways and means Allāh has created and subjected for his use and benefit. This leads him to be humble and grateful to Allāh and to abandon egotism and self-amazement.

This concludes our brief treatment of the six pillars of faith (īmān). A detailed belief in these matters [which cannot be directly seen but are known through strong indirect evidences] increases one's faith. This leads us into the discussion of the relationship between Islām and Īmān and to the nature and reality of faith. This is one of the most crucial aspects to understand about Islām.

## The Reality of Faith

As has preceded, Islām is outward and Īmān (belief, faith) is inward.[40] There is a connection between Islām and Īmān in that the outward Islām *represented by the five pillars* must have a minimal threshhold of inward Īmān for it to be genuine and valid. Likewise, the inward Īmān *represented by the six pillars* must also have a minimal threshhold of outward Islām in word and deed for it to be genuine and valid, and that is **the two testifications and the prayer**.

When the word Islām is used on its own, it refers to the whole religion, inward and outward. Similarly, when Īmān is used on its own, it refers to the whole religion, inward and outward. When they are used together, in the same sentence or context, Islām refers to what is outward and Īmān refers to what is inward.

From the most crucial of affairs that a Muslim must understand is the **binding, necessary, inseparable link** between the internal and the external, between Islām and Īmān, between what is in the heart and what takes place on the tongue and limbs. Anyone who denies this binding link denies what is most elementary, plainly evident and known through the simplest of experiences.

This can be illustrated through the analogy to follow in which attention should be given to:

a) the delivery of knowledge to the heart through the senses,

b) the creation of feelings in the heart through that knowledge,

c) the generation of external actions through those feelings.

As for the analogy:

---

[40] Inward belief is not completely and totally blind—as is commonly understood about "faith"—but rests upon empirical foundations. Belief in Allāh is based upon innate disposition as well as reflection upon the visible traces and effects of His acts of creation, which are readily observed and experienced by all people with their physical senses. Belief in His Books and Messengers is also empirical as they have been seen and heard and first-hand knowledge of them has been authentically transmitted through every generation. As for belief in the Angels, the Last Day, Paradise and Hellfire and matters not sensed or perceived in this world then that is based upon information conveyed through revelation and messengership which is already established through empirical means as has preceded. Thus, faith is not entirely "blind" but does have empirical, evidential basis.

> If we imagine a group of people attending a gathering in a hall within a building in which they enjoy food, drink, make exchanges, engage in trade and shower respect and praise upon each other. A person whom they know well—who is known from past experience to be honest, truthful and reliable and not known to lie or fool around—enters the hall and says, "A raging fire is about to engulf the entire building and you must vacate immediately to escape and be safe". The man also gives instructions so that the people can save themselves from impending danger through a specific, safe and quick route out of the building.

Within this scenario, we can take any person in that gathering and analyse what might take place in his senses, heart and mind of belief and disbelief. This can be explained by the following series of steps:

**First:** The acquisition of sound, authentic information from a known, truthful, trustworthy person not known to lie. It is acquired through hearing and sight and is delivered to the heart and mind. This person may reject the warner and assert he is a liar in which case the truth status of the news imparted by the warner is rejected and knowledge would not have settled in his heart and mind.

**Second:** The nature of this information is not neutral or non-beneficial such that it evokes nothing inside a person of feelings and emotions. It is unlike when a person is informed 2 +2 is 4 or that 1 mile is 1.61 kilometres which is mundane, factual knowledge. So unless a person is deaf, the knowledge so acquired through a truthful channel will stir the heart with emotion and lead to its compliance (inqiyād). Hence, fear (of harm and death), hope (of safety, escape), concern, anxiety, stress, motivation and what is similar will be evoked once this person has mentally understood the words and made minimal reflection upon the knowledge conveyed to him through these words by the honest, truthful warner. The only thing preventing this is if the person was physically deaf, or did not hear, did not understand, or held the warner to be a liar.

**Third:** Such knowledge, feelings and emotions have now been acquired by the heart which would cause it to enter a state of wilful, unhindered compliance (inqiyād). Sound knowledge, accepted as true and factual, creates those feelings and emotions and puts the heart in this state. Unless a person is disabled, lame, or tied in chains, it is a must that this persons stands, speaks and acts. It is not possible for this person to remain sitting unless he or she misunderstood or misheard the truthful informant or holds him to be a liar.

Hence, **action is necessary, it is binding and vital**. A person free of all impediments who is not deaf, disabled, restrained or limited in any way, will stand and act upon the knowledge acquired and upon the emotions necessarily evoked by that knowledge.

The only thing preventing action—if the message was heard and understood perfectly and there were no impediments or restraints—would be pride or arrogance, though it would be seriously out of place in such a situation. Here, a person hates to be commanded and prohibited by another and pride and arrogance prevents him from acting upon the sincere beneficial advice of the truthful warner. In this case, his pride overwhelms and drowns those other feelings which are necessarily produced and he refuses to act, much to his own detriment. He can hear, but is deaf. He can see, but is blind. He has a heart, but it is veiled by his own arrogance. He will suffer, inevitably, the consequences of his arrogance.

This analogy allows us to draw out the nature and reality of Īmān (faith: based upon trust in a truthful source) and kufr (disbelief), and this can be summarised in the following points:

**1. Speech and deed, inward and outward**. Faith comprises both speech and deed and resides in the heart, tongue and limbs. The knowledge (belief) of the heart is its speech. Its feelings and emotions are its actions. The tongue's declaration of belief is its speech. The actions of the limbs include all outward righteous deeds, verbal or physical. As for:

- The claim that faith is only what resides in the heart exclusive to its verbal expression and deeds is false. It is a must that when truthful information comes to the people in the hall gathering that they make verbal expressions and perform actions.

- The claim that faith is verbal expression, exclusive of what is in the heart and performed by the limbs is false. This would turn hypocrites who inwardly disbelieve into true believers.

- The claim that faith comprises what is in the heart and verbal expression exclusive of actions is also false. Actions are a necessity.

Truthful, beneficial knowledge must produce beneficial action. In our analogy of the building and fire, the people must act by necessity.

**Thus, faith is what is in the heart, on the tongue and performed by the limbs.** This is a matter of consensus amongst orthodox Muslim scholars and is based upon a correct understanding of the revealed texts of the Qur'ān and the Prophetic traditions.

Citing this consensus, the Muslim scholar, Abū Bakr al-Ismā'īlī (d. 1059) said: "And they [the orthodox scholars of the Muslims] say: "Certainly, faith is speech (qawl), action ('amal) and belief (ma'rifah). It increases with obedience and decreases with disobedience. He whose obedience increases is more abundant in faith than the one who is less than him in obedience."[41] This nicely introduces our next point.

**2. Increase and decrease.** Faith is liable to increase and decrease. It increases with increase in beneficial knowledge and righteous deeds, whether those of the heart (such as sincerity, love, fear, hope, reliance, humility and so on) or those of the limbs (such as prayer, fasting, charity, truthfulness and so on). It decreases with sins and disobedience. A person's faith can increase until it becomes like mountains and it can also decrease until nothing remains of it save an atom's weight, or even nothing at all.

**3. The binding link between the internal and external.** The actions of the heart are tied to the actions of the limbs, they are the impetus for outward deeds. The outward deeds in turn affect the heart. It is **two way traffic**, the road is in both directions. One affects the other by necessity. Whoever presumes that there can exist perfect faith in the heart without any external manifestation is greatly misguided and has opposed common sense, experience, reason and revelation. Whoever presumes that a person can violate every command and prohibition, without that decreasing—or in some cases negating—the faith in his heart is misguided. This implies that the greatest of sinners and criminals are equal in faith to the most pious.

**3. Levels of faith.** We now understand there are two levels of faith. That which relates to its **validity** (ṣiḥḥah), without which it does not exist, it is the minimal threshold of Islām and Īmān. And that which

---

[41] *I'tiqād A'immat Ahl al-Ḥadīth*. Dār al-Fatḥ (1416H) p. 43.

relates to its **perfection** (kamāl). There are two levels of perfection: **obligatory** (wājib) and **reccommended** (mustaḥabb).

There are obligatory deeds whose neglect makes one sinful and liable to punishment. There are reccommended deeds which perfect one's faith and increase one's rank and reward.[42]

Hence, believers with genuine faith are of three types: Those who wrong themselves by neglecting the obligations and falling into the prohibitions. Those who take a middle course by performing the obligations and keeping away from the prohibitions. Those who are foremost in doing good deeds, who keep the obligations, avoid the prohibitions and perform the voluntary, reccommended deeds whilst avoiding deeds which are disliked, though not forbidden. These three categories are mentioned in the following verse:

ثُمَّ أَوْرَثْنَا الْكِتَابَ الَّذِينَ اصْطَفَيْنَا مِنْ عِبَادِنَا فَمِنْهُمْ ظَالِمٌ لِّنَفْسِهِ وَمِنْهُم مُّقْتَصِدٌ وَمِنْهُمْ سَابِقٌ بِالْخَيْرَاتِ بِإِذْنِ اللَّهِ ذَٰلِكَ هُوَ الْفَضْلُ الْكَبِيرُ

**"Then we caused to inherit the Book those We have chosen of Our servants; and among them is he who wrongs himself, and among them is he who is moderate, and among them is he who is foremost in good deeds by permission of Allāh. That [inheritance of the Book] is indeed the great bounty.**" (35:32).

If faith was just in the heart alone, then all believers, irrespective of their striving, efforts and deeds would be equal and rewarded equally. This is not in agreement with divine justice.

**4. Types of disbelief.** Completing our analogy of the man warning a gathering of people of a fire in the building:

---

[42] It is important to note that whilst deeds are part of and essential to the reality of faith and to salvation, none enters Paradise through deeds alone, but through the grace and mercy of Allāh (عَزَّوَجَلَّ). The Prophet (صَلَّىٱللَّهُعَلَيْهِوَسَلَّمَ) said: "*Be deliberate in worship, draw near to Allāh, and give glad tidings. Verily, none of you will enter Paradise because of his deeds alone.*" They said, "Not even you, O Messenger of Allāh?" The Prophet said: "*Not even me, unless Allāh grants me mercy from himself.*" Related by al-Bukhārī and Muslim. In other words, a person enters Paradise through Allāh's bounty and mercy because Allāh created Him, guided him and gave him the ability and success in performing these deeds which are *a cause* (not the *only cause*) of salvation. Hence, the ultimate cause is Allāh's grace and mercy, and faith in which righteous works are essential, is a requirement.

a) Anyone who considered the truthful warner to be a liar would be a disbeliever. Hence, beneficial knowledge has not settled into the heart and subsequently, the compliance (inqiyād) of the heart will not arise. This would be known as **takdhīb** (rejection).

b) Anyone who was doubtful or hesitant, not knowing whether the warner's message is the truth or not, or whether to act upon it or not, is a disbeliever. It is disbelief of doubt, which is known as **shakk**.

c) Anyone inwardly convinced that the warner is truthful in what he says, but outwardly rejected the information he brought is also a disbeliever, but his disbelief is of a different category. He denies with knowledge. To illustrate, a man borrows money from another and when demanded to repay, he denies he ever borrowed the money. So this is denial after having full knowledge. This is known as **juḥūd**.

d) Anyone who refused to act due to pride and arrogance is also a disbeliever, despite his affirmation of the truthfulness of the warner and the veracity of his information. Thus, not all disbelief relates to the absence of knowledge and belief in the heart alone. Rather, some disbelief is based on the action of the heart alone. This is disbelief of pride and arrogance, which is known as **istikbār**.

e) Anyone who mocked the warner and his message and mocked those who respond to him is also a disbeliever. His disbelief is that of mockery, which is known as **istihzā'**. This is also an action of the heart and is not related to its knowledge and belief. Thus, he might accept the warner is truthful, honest and that his message is true and correct, but nevertheless, mocks the message, belittles it and those who accept and follow it.

f) Anyone who chose not to respond and act in order to remain preoccupied in the gathering and its frivolities is also a disbeliever. Giving preference to worldly pursuits is a barrier to responding to truthful, beneficial knowledge. This is the disbelief of turning away and not caring, which is known as **i'rāḍ**. A person turns away with his hearing, seeing, thinking and reflecting and takes no interest.

g) Anyone who hindered and prevented others from responding to the warner and his message of safety, or worse still, abused them and harmed them is greater in disbelief. This person may, at the same time, know full well that the warner is speaking the truth. Such a heart is filled with hatred, which is known as **kurh**.

The above analogy of the building, the fire and the warner is that of Allāh's Messengers who come to warn and the various responses they receive which divide people into believers and disbelievers, with disbelief being of various types and manifestations.

**In summary**: We have distinguished between Īmān (faith, belief) and what opposes it of disbelief (kufr). We have also explained the nature and reality of faith, how it is a divisible whole, consisting of parts, subject to increase and decrease, being both internal and external, existing in the heart, on the tongue and the limbs. Its parable is like that of a tree which has roots beneath the ground, invisible, just like the heart and what it contains. These roots take nourishment from the soil and water, just like the heart receives beneficial knowledge. In turn these roots nourish what is external, the trunks, branches, twigs and leaves. Similarly, genuine faith in the heart produces external fruits. A condition for the tree's survival and growth in its early life [and eventual bearing of fruits] is the absence of weeds and toxins. Similarly, the heart must be free of beliefs, statements and deeds that clash with faith, harm it and invalidate it.

Thus, the parable:

أَلَمْ تَرَ كَيْفَ ضَرَبَ اللَّهُ مَثَلًا كَلِمَةً طَيِّبَةً كَشَجَرَةٍ طَيِّبَةٍ أَصْلُهَا ثَابِتٌ وَفَرْعُهَا فِي السَّمَاءِ. تُؤْتِي أُكُلَهَا كُلَّ حِينٍ بِإِذْنِ رَبِّهَا وَيَضْرِبُ اللَّهُ الْأَمْثَالَ لِلنَّاسِ لَعَلَّهُمْ يَتَذَكَّرُونَ. وَمَثَلُ كَلِمَةٍ خَبِيثَةٍ كَشَجَرَةٍ خَبِيثَةٍ اجْتُثَّتْ مِن فَوْقِ الْأَرْضِ مَا لَهَا مِن قَرَارٍ

**"See you not how Allāh sets forth a parable of a goodly word as a goodly tree, whose root is firmly fixed, and its branches (reach very hight) to the sky. Giving its fruit at all times, by the leave of its Lord and Allāh sets forth parables for mankind in order that they may remember. And the parable of an evil word is that of an evil tree uprooted from the surface of earth having no stability.**" (14:24-26).

The goodly word is the statement, "*Lā ilāha illallāh*", it is the tree of faith whose roots are firmly established in the heart of a believer. It produces the fruits of sincere, righteous actions which rise up to Allāh and are accepted by Him. The evil word is the statement of disbelief which has no foundation because it is not rooted in observed reality. It is unstable and easily uprooted because it is based upon speculation and nourished by pure conjectures and whims.

## The Pillar of Iḥsān (Excellence)

Islām has three levels.

The first, **Islām**, is entered into through the two testifications and attained through the performance of the most important outward obligations which are its pillars. It is outward and we take everyone who outwardly professes Islām at face value, though Allāḥ knows best what is in the hearts. Outward Islām allows the rulings and rights of other Muslims to take effect.

The second, **Īmān**, is a rank higher than that of Islām and refers to what is in the heart of genuine belief, sincerity, truthfulness, love, humility and so on which must manifest outwardly. Thus a believer increases in beneficial knowledge and righteous action in order to increase his faith, acquire goodness and work towards perfection of character. A believer (muʾmin) is superior than a submitter (muslim), and Allāh knows best what each person is.

The third and highest level is that of **Iḥsān** (excellence) and only has one pillar, which is simple:

**It is to worship Allāh as if you can see Him, but though you cannot see Him, He certainly sees you.**

Such a person is known as a *muḥsin*, or one who excels in good. Such a one possesses the highest rank.

This entails that a person knows that Allāh sees Him no matter where he is or what deed he is engaged in and that he worships Allāh as if he sees Allāh, though he cannot see Allāh.

It is to say and do only that which pleases Allāh.

The fruits of Iḥsān are numerous and include:

a) Cultivation of piety and awareness of Allāh in both the hidden and the open, leading one to become a pious worshipper.

b) Ensuring sincerity to Allāh in one's worship.

c) Winning the nearness, aid and support of Allāh.

d) Succeeding with Paradise in the hereafter.

Allāh (عَزَّوَجَلَّ) said:

هَلْ جَزَاءُ الْإِحْسَانِ إِلَّا الْإِحْسَانُ

**"Is the reward for good [anything] but good?"** (55:60).

## The Three Levels and Ranks

The three levels of Islām have been summarised in a well-known and famous Prophetic tradition. The Prophet's companion, ʿUmar bin al-Khaṭṭāb (رَضِيَ ٱللَّهُ عَنْهُ) related:

"Whilst we were sitting with the Messenger of Allāh (صَلَّى ٱللَّهُ عَلَيْهِ وَسَلَّمَ) one day, there came upon us a man whose clothes were intensely white and whose hair was intensely black. No sign of journey was visible on him and none of us knew him. He came and sat down by the Prophet (صَلَّى ٱللَّهُ عَلَيْهِ وَسَلَّمَ), placing his knees by his (the Prophet's) knees and placed his hands on his thighs.

He said, 'O Muḥammad, inform me about **Islām**.' The Messenger of Allāh said, 'Islām is to bear witness that none has the right to be worshipped but Allāh and Muḥammad is the Messenger of Allāh, to establish the prayer, to pay the zakāh, to fast in Ramaḍān and to make pilgrimage to the House if you are able to do so.' He (the man) said, 'You have spoken truthfully,' and we were amazed at his asking him and confirming he spoke truthfully.

He said, 'Then inform me about **Īmān**.' He said, 'Īmān is to believe in Allāh, His Angels, His Books, His Messengers, the Last Day, and to believe in the Divine Decree.' He said, 'You have spoken truthfully.'

He said, "Then tell me about **Iḥsān**." He said, "It is to worship Allāh as if you can see Him, and even though you cannot see Him, He most certainly sees you."[43]

Muslim scholars throughout the ages have given great attention to this Prophetic tradition and its explanation because it comprises the essence of Islām in a concise and comprehensive way. The contents of this book so far have been an elaboration of this tradition.

The three levels should be considered as three concentric circles. The outermost one is Islām. The middle one is Īmān. The innermost one is Iḥsān. Thereby, every Muḥsin (one who excels) is a Muʾmin (believer) and Muslim (submitter) by default. And every Muʾmin is a Muslim by default. But not every Muslim is a Muʾmin and not every Muʾmin is a Muḥsin.

[43] Related by Muslim in Kitāb al-Īmān.

## Sins and Allāh's Mercy and Forgiveness

It is inevitable that a Muslim has shortcomings and will occasionally fall into sin. Humans have been created with an imperfect nature and are characterised by ignorance (jahl) and oppression (ẓulm). Out of His vast mercy, Allāh (عَزَّوَجَلَّ) has provided ample means through which sins are expiated, erased or forgiven. We shall summarise them here in brief and they are divided into ten categories:[44]

**1. Repentance**. Allāh said:

وَهُوَ الَّذِي يَقْبَلُ التَّوْبَةَ عَنْ عِبَادِهِ وَيَعْفُو عَنِ السَّيِّئَاتِ وَيَعْلَمُ مَا تَفْعَلُونَ

"**And He it is Who accepts repentance from His slaves, and forgives sins, and He knows what you do**." (42:25).

The one who repents from sin is like the one with no sin at all, and the Prophet (صَلَّىٱللَّهُعَلَيْهِوَسَلَّمَ) said: "*All of the Sons of Ādam err and the best of those who err are those who constantly repent*."[45]

**2. Seeking forgiveness**. This is a supplication, a request from Allāh to overlook and pardon one's sin.

وَاسْتَغْفِرُوا رَبَّكُمْ ثُمَّ تُوبُوا إِلَيْهِ إِنَّ رَبِّي رَحِيمٌ وَدُودٌ

"**And ask forgiveness of your Lord and turn unto Him in repentance. Verily, my Lord is Most Merciful, Most Loving.**" (11:90).

Seeking forgiveness is tied with repentance and accompanies it.

**3. Righteous actions**. As stated in the Qurʾān:

إِنَّ الْحَسَنَاتِ يُذْهِبْنَ السَّيِّئَاتِ

"**Verily, the good deeds take away the bad deeds**" (11:114)

The Prophet (صَلَّىٱللَّهُعَلَيْهِوَسَلَّمَ) ordered his companions to follow up bad deeds with good deeds. The regular performance of the obligations, such as prayer, fasting and charity extinguishes sin.

These three categories relate to a person's own deeds. However, Allāh's mercy is greater than that the removal of sins should be tied to a person's own actions alone. Thus:

**4. Supplication of others**. The supplications of believers for each other is from the causes of forgiveness, such as what is done in the funeral prayer wherein Muslims pray and ask for forgiveness for the

---

[44] Refer to Ibn Taymiyyah, *Majmūʿ al-Fatāwā*, 7/487 onwards.
[45] *Ṣaḥīḥ al-Jāmiʿ al-Saghīr* (no. 4515) and it is ḥasan.

deceased. Likewise, whatever supplications they make for each other whether voluntarily or upon request, these supplications aid in the removal of sin from the believers.

**5. Intercession**. The various intercessions by the prophets, angels and righteous that will take place on the Day of Judgement also remove sin. People will be delivered from punishment by way of these intercessions. However, this intercession is only for the people of Tawḥīd, those gave worship exclusively to Allāh alone.

**6. Righteous deeds by others**. Charity, fasting and pilgrimage are righteous deeds that others can do for and on behalf of the deceased and can lead to mercy and forgiveness being granted to him.

These three categories relate to the the deeds of others and are a manifestation of Allāh's mercy upon His servants, He makes it easy for them to acquire forgiveness through many routes. However, Allāh's mercy is greater than that the removal of sins should be tied to the actions of people alone. He also expiates their sins through the trials and tribulations they encounter during their lives.

**7. Worldly afflictions.** A person's sins are expiated through afflictions such as pain, illness, hardship, grief, anxiety and so on, until even the prick of a thorn or a moment of grief expiates sins.

**8. The affliction of the grave**. What takes place in the grave after death also expiates sins. The grave is an intermediate stage between the world and the hereafter and has trials and tribulations which cleanse and purify a believer of his sins.

**9. The trials of the Day of Judgement**. The various hardships and terrors befalling on that day also expiate and remove sins.

These three relate to the various calamities a person faces in the three abodes: *the world*, *the grave* and *the hereafter*. However, Allāh's mercy is greater than that it should be tied only to the ways and means which He placed, whether legislative or creative. Thus:

**10. Allāh's mercy**. There is still left, the pure mercy of Allāh—not tied to any causes or means—through which He forgives whomever He wills. A person may still come with sins like mountains after all of the above, yet Allāh may choose to forgive him. The only condition is that he meets Allāh whilst not associating any partners with Him in worship. This shows the greatness of the affair of Tawḥīd. However, alongside this, one does not forget or belittle the affair of sin.

## The Nullifiers of Islām

We have discussed sins which a Muslim must not take lightly, even if the ways and means for their forgiveness are many. While it is true that Allāh is most-Merciful, vast and overflowing in His mercy, it is not permissible for a Muslim to simply hope in Allāh's mercy alone and indulge in sins without care or concern, without fearing His punishment. Hence, he or she must combine between hoping in Allāh's mercy and fearing His punishment. They are like the two wings of a bird, without one or the other, there will be problems. In a like manner, a worshipper cannot travel to his Lord through hope *alone* as this leads to unfounded optimism, or through fear *alone* as this leads to unfounded despair, but must combine them together in order to remain stable, both inwardly and outwardly.

The next extremely important matter to grasp is that a Muslim can leave Islām through beliefs, statements and deeds that clash with the foundations of Islām and cannot be reconciled with it.

Here we present a list of affairs that are mutually exclusive with Islām, clashing with faith and its foundations from every angle. These affairs are agreed upon by Muslim scholars from the well-known orthodox schools of jurisprudence and are not in dispute. To protect and preserve one's Islām, a Muslim must learn these affairs and be cautious with respect to them.

These affairs are:

**1. Associating partners with Allāh.** Worshipping others alongside Allāh, praying to them, sacrificing to them, seeking rescue from them, asking them for things only Allāh has power and control over, all of this directly contradicts Islām and violates Tawḥīd.

It is not possible for a person to say, "*None has the right to be worshipped but Allāh alone*" and then worship others besides Him. His statement is of no effect. It is no different to a person claiming to be a vegetarian and being committed to vegetarianism but who regularly eats beef burgers. This is impossible by definition. Hence, the claim that one can profess Islām and then say and do *whatever* one likes is false and is only said by the ignoramus or the one desiring to negate Islām from its very foundations.

Allāh (عَزَّوَجَلَّ) said:

إِنَّ اللَّهَ لَا يَغْفِرُ أَن يُشْرَكَ بِهِ وَيَغْفِرُ مَا دُونَ ذَٰلِكَ لِمَن يَشَاءُ

**"Verily, Allāh forgives not that partners should be set up with him in worship, but He forgives besides that [anything else] to whom He pleases."** (4:48).

**2. Setting up intermediaries.** Setting up intermediaries in order to take them as intercessors such that one asks from Allāh through them, invokes them, places one's reliance upon them and uses them as a means of nearness to Allāh and as a means of repelling harms, acquiring benefits and acquiring that which only Allāh has power over, such as the forgiveness of sins, entry into Paradise, removal of sickness and the likes. All of this invalidates Islām.

Allāh (عَزَّوَجَلَّ) said:

وَيَعْبُدُونَ مِن دُونِ اللَّهِ مَا لَا يَضُرُّهُمْ وَلَا يَنفَعُهُمْ وَيَقُولُونَ هَٰؤُلَاءِ شُفَعَاؤُنَا عِندَ اللَّهِ قُلْ أَتُنَبِّئُونَ اللَّهَ بِمَا لَا يَعْلَمُ فِي السَّمَاوَاتِ وَلَا فِي الْأَرْضِ سُبْحَانَهُ وَتَعَالَىٰ عَمَّا يُشْرِكُونَ

**"And they worship besides Allāh that which neither harms them nor benefits them, and they say, 'These are our intercessors with Allāh.' Say, 'Do you inform Allāh of something He does not know in the Heavens or on the Earth?' Exalted is He and high above what they associate with Him."** (10:18).

The route to Allāh is direct and unhindered, without barriers and gateways. One can ask directly from Allāh rather than through a multitude of intercessors.[46] The Christians worship saints, take them as intermediaries and intercessors and invoke them for needs which can only be fulfilled by Allāh. Unfortunately, many Muslims have followed in their footsteps and have taken the inhabitants of graves as objects of reverence and worship, invoking them alongside Allāh. This matter has even become widespread in many of the Muslim

---

[46] As for asking a living person to supplicate to Allāh for you, it is from the permitted ways and means. Likewise, asking a living, present, hearing, able person to do something for you for which he has the power and ability in the worldly affairs, this is also permissible.

lands, which helps to explain their weakness, subjugation and humiliation among the nations.

**3. Validating false religion**. Considering the way of those who worship stones, trees, idols, humans, angels, jinn, the elements and so on, to comprise legitimate religion and alternative, acceptable ways to Allāh is also a nullifier of Islām. This is a belief that invalidates the truth of the statement, "*None has the right to be worshipped but Allāh alone*". Rather, a Muslim must free himself from false religion and hold it to be incorrect and futile. Allāh (عَزَّوَجَلَّ) said:

وَمَن يَبْتَغِ غَيْرَ الْإِسْلَامِ دِينًا فَلَن يُقْبَلَ مِنْهُ وَهُوَ فِي الْآخِرَةِ مِنَ الْخَاسِرِينَ

"**And whoever seeks a religion other than Islām, it will never be accepted of him, and in the Hereafter he will be of the losers**." (3:85).

This does not prevent a Muslim from having just behaviour and conduct with non-Muslims. A Muslim does not compromise with the truth, nor does he engage in injustice towards others. Rather, he is obligated to be just towards them and is permitted to be benevolent and kind to those who do not fight, wrong or harm him.

**4. Believing another guidance is better**. To believe that there is a guidance more truthful, more beneficial, and more excellent than the guidance taught by the Prophets and Messengers, at the head of them and the very last of them, Muḥammad (صَلَّىٱللَّهُعَلَيْهِوَسَلَّمَ). The best guidance is that of Muḥammad (صَلَّىٱللَّهُعَلَيْهِوَسَلَّمَ), it is a culmination and perfection of the guidance of Noah, Abraham, Moses and Jesus (عَلَيْهِمُٱلسَّلَامُ). It guides to the truth and that which is upright in morals and conduct. Its rulings protect and preserve the necessities of **life**, **property**, **reason**, **lineage** and **honour** in a manner unrivalled by any other legislation.

Allāh (عَزَّوَجَلَّ) said:

اللَّهُ نَزَّلَ أَحْسَنَ الْحَدِيثِ كِتَابًا مُّتَشَابِهًا مَّثَانِيَ تَقْشَعِرُّ مِنْهُ جُلُودُ الَّذِينَ يَخْشَوْنَ رَبَّهُمْ ثُمَّ تَلِينُ جُلُودُهُمْ وَقُلُوبُهُمْ إِلَىٰ ذِكْرِ اللَّهِ ذَٰلِكَ هُدَى اللَّهِ يَهْدِي بِهِ مَن يَشَاءُ وَمَن يُضْلِلِ اللَّهُ فَمَا لَهُ مِنْ هَادٍ

"**Allāh has sent down the best statement, a Book (this Qur'ān), its parts resembling each other in goodness and oft-repeated t ruth. The skins of those who fear their Lord shiver from it [when they recite it**

**or hear it]. Then their skins and hearts soften to the remembrance of Allāh. That is the guidance of Allāh. He guides therewith whom He pleases and whomever Allah sends astray, for him there is no guide.**" (39:23).

**5. Hating anything the Messenger came with.** Hating the truth brought by the Messengers, and at the head of them Muḥammad (ﷺ), or hating any aspect or element of it invalidates Islām. For example, to hate and dislike the prayer, or zakāt (obligatory charity), or the commands in Islām which relate to maintaining modesty and chastity, or any of its legislations, invalidates Islām. Hatred in the heart cannot be reconciled with the acceptance (qabūl) and compliance (inqiyād) of the heart. Hence, a Muslim must submit and accept all of the truth. There may be things which a person may not understand, whose wisdom may not be clear and which may be contrary to habit, custom, or one's limited reason. However, a person should not harbour hatred and dislike, rather he or she must gain more knowledge and acquire clarification and understanding if able, and if not, then to submit, acknowledge one's own limitations and keep the heart safe and sound. Allāh (عَزَّوَجَلَّ) said:

ذَٰلِكَ بِأَنَّهُمْ كَرِهُوا مَا أَنزَلَ اللَّهُ فَأَحْبَطَ أَعْمَالَهُمْ

**"That is because they hate that which Allāh has sent down (of this Qur'ān and its rules and injunctions), so He has made their deeds to be fruitless."** (47:9)

**6. Mocking or belittling Islām or anything from it.** Mocking and belittling Islām or anything from its laws, or mocking the Prophet (ﷺ) and belittling him is an automatic nullifier of Islām. Such mockery and belittlement which emanates from the heart cannot be reconciled with the respect, veneration, love and compliance that emanates through the knowledge that it is truth from the Lord of the worlds. Since Muslims believe in the existence of absolute truth and falsehood, guidance and misguidance, then there are sanctities that cannot be violated and boundaries which cannot be overstepped. This is unlike secular, liberal, atheist philosophies in which there is no intrinsic, inherent purpose to life [and thus no absolute truth] and everyone must invent and pursue his own meaning and purpose in life whilst being allowed to make fun of everyone else's, because, ultimately, there are no sanctities. However, Muslims do not believe that the Heavens, the Earth and life therein is in vain. Rather, there is an absolute truth and there will be absolute justice. Hence, there are sanctities which cannot be violated, otherwise truth is undermined and eroded. Thus, any Muslim who mocked Islam, or anything from it, or who mocked the Messenger (ﷺ) has invalidated his Islām, because through this mockery or belittlement a person has emptied his heart of love, compliance, veneration and respect.

Allāh (عَزَّوَجَلَّ) said regarding a group of hypocrites who made fun of the Prophet and his companions on account of religion:

وَلَئِن سَأَلْتَهُمْ لَيَقُولُنَّ إِنَّمَا كُنَّا نَخُوضُ وَنَلْعَبُ قُلْ أَبِاللَّهِ وَآيَاتِهِ وَرَسُولِهِ كُنتُمْ تَسْتَهْزِئُونَ. لَا تَعْتَذِرُوا قَدْ كَفَرْتُم بَعْدَ إِيمَانِكُمْ

**"If you ask them, they declare: 'We were only talking idly and joking.' Say: 'Was it at Allāh, and His signs and His Messenger that you were mocking?' Make no excuse; you have disbelieved after your belief.**" (9:65-66).

The Muslim scholar Shaykh al-Saʿdī (d. 1956) said: "Making fun of Allāh and His Messenger is disbelief which expels from the religion. This is because the foundation of religion is built upon venerating Allāh, His religion and His messengers. Mocking anything from that negates this foundation and invalidates it in the most severe way."[47]

Thus mocking the beard for men, or mocking the women's hijāb, or mocking the prayer or the pilgrimage or anything known from Islām through authentic texts is disbelief.

**7. Practising magic**. Magic is a mutually beneficial relationship between men and devils (jinn)[48] in which magicians obey the

---

[47] *Taysīr al-Karīm al-Raḥmān Fī Tafsīr Kalām al-Mannān*. Beirūt: Risālah Publishers (1423H), pp. 342-343.

[48] The jinn are created beings and, like angels, cannot be seen by men in their original form. They were created before men from the smokeless flame-material of fire and are obligated to respond to the Prophets. They are also punished and rewarded. In general, the jinn live in remote areas, away from the habitations of men. Jinn can affect, influence and possess men and

demands of the devils and the devils fulfil the requests of magicians. The magic being referred to is that in which the assistance of the devils is sought in order to effect some benefit or harm in others, and not the tricks and illusions performed by mere sleight of hand, advanced knowledge of mechanisms and use of devices with no involvement from the devils. The devils do not assist magicians until and unless they commit disbelief through speech or deed. As such, disbelief is an automatic presumption in all devil-assisted magic. Anyone engaging in this magic has invalidated his Islām, even if he professes Islām outwardly and appears as a pious worshipper.

Allāh (عَزَّوَجَلَّ) said about those who purchase magic, denying that they have any share in the hereafter, proving their disbelief:

وَيَتَعَلَّمُونَ مَا يَضُرُّهُمْ وَلَا يَنفَعُهُمْ وَلَقَدْ عَلِمُوا لَمَنِ اشْتَرَاهُ مَا لَهُ فِي الْآخِرَةِ مِنْ خَلَاقٍ

وَلَبِئْسَ مَا شَرَوْا بِهِ أَنفُسَهُمْ لَوْ كَانُوا يَعْلَمُونَ

**"But they certainly knew that whoever purchased magic would not have in the Hereafter any share. And wretched is that for which they sold themselves, if they only knew."** (2:102).

Magicians profit from the events, circumstances or misfortunes in the lives of others in which there are interplays of greed, lust, jealousy and the seeking of revenge, fame, authority and power. These are the evils and poisons of the heart. The magicians exploit these base desires in people by offering assistance to them in achieving their goals. This assistance is provided through the devils. To win it, the magicians willingly engage in statements or deeds of disbelief or polytheism. Examples include mocking Allāh, writing on the Qurʾān with menstrual blood, throwing the Qurʾān into filth, sacrificing a chicken or lamb to the devils, worshipping idols and other such evil, repugnant actions. The magicians embezzle wealth from people by offering them help in their personal lives and in the predicaments they find themselves in. In reality they are corrupters of society and engage in the vilest of professions, selling themselves for a paltry, miserable price, and only cause harm, not rectification.

---

this is known empirically and through experience. Different societies and civilisations have invented mythologies, names, labels and titles to explain a variety of phenomena that actually arise due to the jinn.

It is a rule that whenever tawḥīd (monotheism) and īmān (faith) are rooted within a society, the magicians hide and go underground. And whenever polytheism, disbelief and ignorance are widespread, the magicians surface and become widespread.[49]

**8. Aiding polytheists against Muslims**. Aiding polytheists and disbelievers against Muslims due to having love for the religion of the polytheists and out of the desire to see it dominate over the religion of the Muslims is an obvious nullifier of Islām. It is not possible for there to be inward faith in the presence of such an action.

The Muslim scholars have discussed and clarified the matter of loyalty and allegiance in a detailed manner and we provide a concise summary here:

a) A Muslim may love, respect and honour his or her non-Muslim Jewish or Christian spouse, non-Muslim parents of any background, non-Muslim sons and daughters or non-Muslim relatives. He or she may respect and show kindness to non-Muslim neighbours. A Muslim does not love, honour and respect these categories of people out of love for their religion but because of specific worldly relationships in which love or respect is natural. Honouring them or showing kindness to them is enjoined in Islām.

b) A Muslim might show love and loyalty to a non-Muslim (outside of the first category above), because of some worldly benefit he seeks to gain *at the expense of neglecting some aspects or elements of his religion.* This is considered a sin and prohibited because it is an impermissible compromise. A Muslim must be more honourable than to try and acquire worldly benefits in such a manner.

c) A Muslim might show love, loyalty, allegiance and aid to the polytheists and disbelievers due to their religion. In other words, he loves them for their religion and aids them against the Muslims. He wants them to dominate the Muslims and for their religion to be strengthened against that of the Muslims. This nullifies Islām without

---

[49] In a like manner, whenever Islām and its injunctions are rooted within a society, the nation-destroyers such as usury, alcohol, gambling and fornication or adultery are absent or minimised. These affairs destroy life, lineage, intellect and property which Islām came to protect vigorously. And whenever a society is far from Islām, these destroyers take root.

any doubt and clashes with faith from every angle. As for when he aids and supports them for a worldly reason, not out of love for their religion, then this is a very serious major sin.

These are very important distinctions which must be understood especially in these times in which we have a) *extremists and terrorists* who are engaged in a war against Islām and Muslims before anyone else[50] and b) *liberals* following their desires who wish to rewrite and undermine Islām from its very foundations and destroy the distinct, noble, honourable identity of true, upright Muslims.[51]

**9. Believing one is exempt from following the Prophet (ﷺ).** The claim that there are people who are exempt from following the guidance of the Prophet (ﷺ) is disbelief and invalidates a person's Islām. This belief is found among some extreme sects such as those among the Ṣūfīs[52] who claim that there are certain people who receive illumination from Allāh directly and no longer need to follow the Prophet and his guidance because it is only for the common people and not for the elite like them. They claim that their saints or

---

[50] Due to their severe ignorance and complete lack of understanding of basic principles of Islāmic law, the extremists and terrorists accuse rulers, governments of Muslim countries and their institutions such as the military and police of apostasy because of permissible diplomatic and trade relations with non-Muslim nations.

[51] Many so-called liberals claiming to "reform" Islām manifest the signs and characteristics of hypocrites and their claim to Islām is questionable.

[52] Ṣūfism is an innovated tradition influenced by Gnosticism, Greek philosophy (neo-Platonism) and aspects of Buddhism. It is alluring and appealing to those who are not well-informed because of its apparent association with spirituality and purification of the soul. However, there are doctrines one is lead to through this deceptive door which clash with Islām and constitute a form of disbelief greater than that of the Christians who said God indwells within Jesus. Such doctrines include that of the unity of existence (*waḥdat al-wujūd*) in which it is claimed that there is no existence save that of God, there is no such thing as "creator" or "created" and that everything is a physical manifestation of the divine essence. These doctrines appeared amongst the Muslims after mixing with the nations and being influenced by foreign ideological poisons.

The best guidance is the guidance of Muḥammad (ﷺ) and what he legislated and commanded of affairs pertaining to the purification of the soul is sufficient for the attainment of inward and outward perfection.

elites can bypass the Prophets and Messengers and receive sudden illumination (kashf) and guidance directly from Allāh. This is plain disbelief and a clear invalidation of the statement: "Muḥammad (ﷺ) is the Messenger of Allāh."

From the devices used by these people to misguide others is that they divide the religion into what they call the **apparent** (ẓāhir) or the **external law** (sharīʿah) on the one hand, which they claim is for the shallow, unsophisticated commoners. And on the other hand, the **hidden** (bāṭin) or the **inner reality** (ḥaqīqah) which refers to secret doctrines and interpretations and is only for the philosophical elite who are able to grasp higher truths, unlike those inferior to them. By mystifying religion in this way and claiming their leaders possess secret knowledge, they lay down foundations for the development of cults and cult ideologies. There is no path to Allāh except through the Prophet (ﷺ) whose guidance is a completion and perfection of the guidance of all the Prophets and Messengers sent by Allāh. There is no *hidden knowledge*, *secret organisation* or *elitism* in Islām. Rather, these matters are the foundation of misguidance.

**10. Turning away from Islām**. To turn away *entirely* from Islām after professing it and not having any desire at all to learn or act upon it, to turn one's back on obedience to Allāh and His Messenger, to choose to remain ignorant of the foundations by which one's Islām and Īmān are kept intact despite having the means and ability to learn them, all of this this nullifies Islām. It is impossible for a person to believe in his heart and express with his tongue yet not perform a single outward obligation in his life, ever. It is impossible for a person who has professed Islām to have no desire at all to learn that by which he fulfils his most basic obligations. Whoever turns away completely with his hearing, seeing, heart and body from Islām in this manner cannot remain a Muslim, indicating the great danger of having no desire at all for knowledge and action.

To conclude this chapter, a Muslim must take caution with respect to this serious topic. He or she must study the nature and reality of faith (īmān) and the various beliefs, statements and actions that diminish it or nullify it altogether.

## Perfection of Morals and Character

The two testifications of **Islām** comprise the essential message of all previous prophets and messengers. The declaration which enters a person into Islām, has a **meaning** (maʿnā), **requirements** (muqtaḍā), **conditions** (shurūṭ) and **nullifiers** (nawāqiḍ).

After a person enters Islām, he establishes the remaining pillars and seeks knowledge to increase inward **Īmān** (faith). Thereafter, he strives for **Iḥsān** (excellence). All the while, he remains fearful and cautious lest his faith diminish due to sins or even disappear due to various nullifiers. To attain excellence and perfection, he or she must aim to emulate the Prophet (ﷺ) in his qualities and traits of perfection, from them:

**- Pure monotheism in belief, speech and deed**
- Kindness, benevolence - Sincerity - Rectifying affairs
- Reflecting - Spreading abundant salutations of peace
- Eating from the wholesome and pure - Spending upon others
- Trustworthiness, fulfilling one's trusts - Justice in dealings
- Being penitent - Insightfulness and perspicacity - Humility
- Righteousness - Benevolence - Kindness to one's parents
- Having a good countenance, being cheerful
- Weeping out of humility and piety - Repentance
- Cooperating upon righteousness - *Honouring the mother*
- Venerating that which is sacred and inviolable
- Piety - Recitation of the Qur'ān - Pondering deeply
- Reliance - Generosity - Good manners
- Adopting legislated ways and means to pursue livelihood
- Reflective silence - Forbearance - Serenity
- Excellent behaviour and dealings with one's family
- Modesty, shyness - Guarding chastity - *Honouring the mother*
- Invocation, supplication - Frequent remembrance of Allāh
- Showing mercy to others - Gentleness - Gratitude - Patience
- Charity - Abstinence from what is non-beneficial
- Truthfulness - Abundant prayer - *Honouring the mother*
- Maintaining family ties - Being organised
- Guarding one's tongue from what is indecent, immoral
- Fasting - Maintaining bodily cleanliness and purity

- Firm determination and resolve
- Proceeding upon knowledge - Having certainty
- Lofty intentions and objectives - Being charitable
- Being diligent - Visiting the sick - Remembrance of death
- Astuteness - Comprehension - Bravery
- Nobility - Looking after the widow and the orphan
- Struggling against one's soul in obedience to Allāh
- Accounting one's soul - Giving sincere advice

and many other traits all of which are manifest in the person and character of Muḥammad (ﷺ), as stated in the Qur'ān:

وَإِنَّكَ لَعَلَىٰ خُلُقٍ عَظِيمٍ

"**And certainly, you [O Muḥammad] are upon an exalted standard of character.**" (68:4).

From the many statements of the Prophet Muḥammad (ﷺ) strongly emphasising the position of lofty manners and nobility in Islām:

"*I was not sent [as a Messenger] but to perfect the righteous, beneficial traits (qualities, manners, behaviours).*"[53] "*[The whole of ] righteousness is [but] noble manners.*"[54] "*There is nothing placed on the scales [of righteous deeds] weightier than good manners.*"[55] "*The most perfect of believers in faith are the best of them in manners, and the best of you are those best in their manners to their wives.*"[56] "*Indeed, the best of you are those who are best in manners.*"[57] Explaining that which enters people into Paradise most: "*Reverential fear (taqwā) of Allāh and good manners.*"[58] "*I will be an advocate for a house in the highest part in Paradise for the one who exemplifies the best of manners.*"[59]

This is only a small selection out of a large number of narrations that establish the utmost importance of perfection of morals and character in Islām.

---

[53] Ṣaḥīḥ al-Jāmiʿ al-Ṣaghīr (no. 2349).
[54] Related by Muslim (no. 4633).
[55] Ṣaḥīḥ al-Targhīb wal-Tarhīb (no. 2641).
[56] Ṣaḥīḥ al-Jāmiʿ al-Ṣaghīr (no. 1232).
[57] Related by al-Bukhārī (no. 5569).
[58] Ṣaḥīḥ al-Targhīb wal-Tarhīb (no. 2642).
[59] Ṣaḥīḥ al-Targhīb wal-Tarhīb (no. 2648).

## Preservation of Islām, Īmān and Iḥsān

We have now completed our presentation of Islām through its **three levels**. We have explained the clear and **definitive boundaries** that separate Islām and Īmān from whatever clashes with and invalidates them. Also mentioned was the great importance of working towards **perfection and nobility in character** based upon a firm and stable foundation which is:

- belief in Allāh and **His unique oneness**,
- then **loving** Him for His innumerable favours and bounties,
- and upon that, **worshipping Him alone**,
- while **fearing** His displeasure and punishment,
- and **hoping** for His pleasure and reward.

All human behaviour is motivated and driven by *love*, *hope* and *fear*. No wilfully chosen action from any person ever falls outside of these three. These three emotions can be rooted in falsehood and incoherent, irrational beliefs or they can be rooted in truth and a coherent, rational, warranted belief. A firm, lasting, ethical and moral order that returns tangible benefits in the interests of **both the individual and the society** can only be based upon firm foundations that are rooted in truth and justice.[60]

Islām cultivates excellent morals, lofty manners and righteous conduct so that all those beneficial interests whose attainment makes societies thrive and prosper can be more easily extracted from the *goldmine* of human capital. **Humans are potential goldmines** and

---

[60] It is for this reason that Muslim societies adhering to Islām are more resilient to subversion and not easily exploited through usury, alcohol, gambling, drugs, fornication and adultery by which private interests benefit financially through the manipulation of base human desires. This is because Muslims have a law founded upon pure monotheism which protects all beneficial interests—both spiritual and material—of the individual and society. Thus, such nation-destroying evils are not allowed to take root. In contrast Christian societies followed Pauline Christianity which abolished the law and restricted faith to beliefs in triads and trinities, personal saviours and other pagan-originating concepts that clash with the genuine teachings of Jesus: believing in one Lord, worshipping Him alone, and observing the law by combining inward faith with outward deeds. For that reason, Christian nations and societies are not resilient to erosion and subversion because they are devoid of a truth-based protective law.

nobility and excellence can be cultivated and extracted out of them, but only with guidance that combines between beneficial knowledge and righteous action. Islām provides that guidance and its route is the revealed books and sent messengers, the last of which are the Qur'ān and the Prophet Muḥammad (صَلَّى ٱللَّٰهُ عَلَيْهِ وَسَلَّمَ).

Having said this, there are threats to the beneficial interests of the individual and the society. These threats operate at the individual level, affecting a person's inward and outward faith, and in turn, affect the well-being of the society at the wider level.

The best way to illustrate them is through a parable which can serve as a conceptual framework for practical action based upon the sum of what has preceded.

### A Parable for One's Faith (Īmān)

Imagine you are holding **a tank of water** with both of your hands as you traverse on a journey in which the collection and preservation of water determines your survival. **Five dangers** to the amount and purity of the water exist from the **environment** and the **people** surrounding you, and they are placed in a specific order:

a) *Spilling* of some of the water in small or large amounts.
b) A change in the water's *colour* through impurities.
c) A change in the water's *odour* through impurities.
d) A change in the waters' *taste* through impurities.
e) Tripping or falling and *complete loss* of the water.

The water is your **Īmān**. The vessel is your **heart**. Your aim is to gather **pure water** through rain, fresh streams and the likes so that your tank becomes full. You drink the clean water and it keeps you alive, breathing, speaking and acting. Similarly, **Īmān** (faith)—*acquired through authentic revealed knowledge*—keeps your heart alive, knowing, remembering, worshipping, acting and so on.

However, you must avoid the five dangers which harm, poison, spoil, spill or empty the water altogether from your tank. When you slip (sin), you lose some of the water through spillage. Things can be slipped into your tank with or without your knowledge and spoil the water in its colour (making it unpleasant to look at), odour (make it unpleasant to smell) and taste (make it repugnant to drink). The same can happen to Īmān in your heart through doubts, innovations, misconceptions, heresies, lusts and desires. It can be spoiled and corrupted. There are also the hateful and spiteful who want you to lose your water altogether. They try to deceive you into pouring it out. Or they put obstacles in your way to make you fall and lose it all. If unable, they poison it. These are the people who want you to lose your Īmān completely or to wilfully abandon it altogether. They are driven by material or ideological interests.

Your aim is to keep filling your tank till it becomes full and to remain cautious and in perfect balance to avoid **spillage**, **spoilage** and **sackage**. Let us explain each of these three dangers.

### Spillage.

Faith (Īmān) is like a substance which is fluid and divisible, hence the parable with water. You spill water every time you slip. When you sin, some faith is lost through spillage, just like water is lost every time you slip. A sin is disobedience of Allāh's command.

Out of His perfect knowledge and wisdom, Allāh only commands what is beneficial for both the individual and the society and only prohibits what is harmful for them.

Allāh has rights over your body and wealth; your body has rights over you; and Allāh's servants have rights over each other. When you sin, you are violating the right of Allāh to be obeyed and you are violating the right of your soul and body to be kept in compliance with Allāh's command. If your sin entails harm to others in their property, person or honour, you have added violation of the rights of Allāh's servants to the first two violations.

Through these violations, the individual and society is harmed, leading to corruption. Allāh (عَزَّوَجَلَّ) said:

إِنَّ اللَّهَ يَأْمُرُ بِالْعَدْلِ وَالْإِحْسَانِ وَإِيتَاءِ ذِي الْقُرْبَىٰ وَيَنْهَىٰ عَنِ الْفَحْشَاءِ وَالْمُنكَرِ وَالْبَغْيِ يَعِظُكُمْ لَعَلَّكُمْ تَذَكَّرُونَ

**"Indeed, Allāh orders justice and good conduct and giving to relatives and forbids immorality and bad conduct and oppression. He admonishes you that perhaps you will be reminded.**" (16:90).

The Muslim scholar, Shaykh ʿAbd al-Raḥmān al-Saʿdī (d. 1956) said of this verse: "This verse has comprehensively incorporated all the commands and prohibitions, nothing remains except that it enters into this [verse]. It is a principle to which all the details [of law] return. Every affair comprising justice, good conduct and generosity is from that which Allāh has commanded. Every affair comprising indecency, evil conduct and injustice is from that which Allāh has prohibited."[61] All sins are *indecency, harmful conduct* or *injustice.*

**Sins can be major and minor.** Major sins lead to great spillage and minor sins lead to less spillage, though they can add up and become equivalent to the effect of major sins if one belittles them. Major sins impact **the five necessities** which are preservation of: a) *sound religion*, b) *life*, c) *wealth*, d) *intellect* and e) *lineage or honour*. So long as one avoids the major sins, the minor sins will be erased:

إِن تَجْتَنِبُوا كَبَائِرَ مَا تُنْهَوْنَ عَنْهُ نُكَفِّرْ عَنكُمْ سَيِّئَاتِكُمْ وَنُدْخِلْكُم مُّدْخَلًا كَرِيمًا

**"If you avoid the major sins which you are forbidden, We will remove from you your lesser sins and admit you to a noble entrance [into Paradise]."**(4:31).

Thus, a Muslim must not to treat sin lightly because its evil effects return back to himself and to the society. Cause-effect mechanisms exist in the realm of human actions just as they exist in the realm of nature. They are explained in revealed knowledge and cannot always be determined through reflection, science or short-term experiences, unless long-term direct observations of human activity and its effects are made over centuries or longer.

For example, it is mentioned in authentic Prophetic traditions that open lewdness leads to spread of sexual diseases; that cheating in weights and measures leads to economic hardships and tyranny of rulers; that withholding obligatory charity leads to droughts; that being content with the world, dealing in forbidden transactions and not striving in Allāh's cause leads to humiliation of Muslim societies and nations; that violating Tawḥīd and leaving Prophetic guidance leads to subjugation and plunder by enemies. Many correlations can be found in the Qur'ān and Prophetic traditions between human acts and negative, harmful consequences.

Thus, one should not belittle the affair of sin, because everything Allāh has prohibited brings harm to the individual and the society.

---

[61] *Taysīr al-Karīm al-Raḥmān* (Beirut: Muʿassasah al-Risālah, 2002) p. 477.

Allāh gains nothing and loses nothing from His servants if they choose to sin, the harms only return upon them. Thus, the first goal is to prevent as much spillage as possible, both major and minor.

**Spoilage.**

Water can be spoiled in terms of its *colour*, *odour* and *taste*. Faith can be spoiled through desires, which are sins, they relate **to matters of action, whether of the hearts or limbs**. Sins cause spillage as has preceded and every instance of sin has a *spoiling effect* on whatever remains. The more one indulges in sin, the more discolouration, distaste and malodour takes place in the water (faith). But more serious is that faith can also be spoiled through desires of another kind, which are more harmful than the ones just discussed.

They are **heresies and innovations** and relate to **matters of knowledge and worship**. They are more harmful than sins because when a person sins, he knows wrong has been committed. A person never take sin as a path to be followed in religion. No one says, "My path in religion is to drink, steal, murder, gamble and fornicate". But with heresies and innovations, once a person falls into them, he will consider them to be truth and guidance. A person's faith can be corrupted and spoiled through false, heretical doctrines, innovated forms of worship and methodologies. He or she takes them as a path to be followed in religion. The Prophet (صَلَّى ٱللَّهُ عَلَيْهِ وَسَلَّمَ) prophesied that the fate of previous nations of differing and division will happen to the Muslim nation. He said: "*The Jews split into 71 sects, the Christians split into 72 sects, and this nation will split into 73 sects*."[62]

Due to the factors of: influences from other nations;[63] ignorance of texts; specific political circumstances; and the activities of hypocrites and subversives, numerous ideas crept into the Muslim nation through certain individuals. They tried to reconcile them with the revealed texts, leading to innovations and heresies, and then became callers to these doctrines in the name of Islām. This led to the emergence of sects and the splitting of the Muslim nation.

---

[62] *Ṣaḥīḥ Sunan Abī Dāwūd* (no. 4596) and *Ṣaḥīḥ Sunan al-Tirmidhī* (no. 2640).

[63] Such as the Jews, Christians, Sabeans, Greeks, Hindus and Buddhists. As Islām spread to distant lands, the prior doctrinal baggage of nations helped to shape new, innovated ideas that were ascribed to Islām and its texts.

These sects and their ideas—despite appearing so long ago—continue to exist today. They may not be readily identified because often names and labels change though the realities remain the same. Here are the main sects to appear in the history of Islām:

**1. Khārijites:** They are the precursors to modern-day extremist and terrorist groups such as al-Qaeda, ISIS (Daesh), Boko Haram and others. They appeared due to discontent in material matters and revolted against the Muslim rulers whom they accused of not judging by justice. They later judged those who commit sins to be disbelievers and claimed they will reside eternally in the Hellfire. They killed two of the greatest companions of the Prophet (ﷺ), ʿUthmān and ʿAlī (رَضِيَ ٱللَّهُ عَنْهُمَا), the third and fourth caliphs of Islām respectively. They oppressively justify the killing of Muslim men, women and children. Their continued appearance within the Muslim nation was foretold by the Prophet in many authentic traditions who described them as "*the most evil of creation*" and "*dogs of hellfire*". They are *zealous yet ignorant* revolutionaries whom the leaders of the Muslims are ordered to fight when they manifest their evil. A Muslim does not leave Islām on account of major sins, but his faith becomes deficient. A ruler is not expelled from Islām if he does not judge with justice nor is he to be rebelled against. This is prohibited in order to preserve stability and safety and prevent greater evils from engulfing the society. As for the Khārijites, they destroy the worldly affairs and spread fear.

**2. Shīʿites:** They exaggerated the status of ʿAlī, the fourth caliph and cousin of the Prophet, and claimed he was the rightful heir to political leadership after the Prophet. Then ʿAlī was claimed to have been the intended recipient of the Qur'ān instead of Muḥammad (ﷺ). Then he was claimed to have been inhabited by the "Spirit of God". Finally, he was claimed to have been God himself similar to how the Christians claimed God became incarnate in Jesus (عَلَيْهِ ٱلسَّلَامُ).

They claimed that the Qur'ān has hidden, esoteric meanings known only to ʿAlī and his offspring and that true Islām could only be known and conveyed through their lineage. They declared virtually all of the Prophet's companions to be disbelievers and slandered the wives of the Prophet (ﷺ). Many secretive, esoteric movements adopted the face of Shīʿism as a veil to infiltrate Islām and its people.[64] Today, the main body of Shīʿites is concentrated in Irān—formerly **Zoroastrian Persia**—which has proxies in the Sunnī lands. The Scholars of Islām do not consider anyone who believes in these doctrines to be a Muslim. From the great foundations of Islām is to love, respect and honour the members of the Prophet's household which includes his wives and likewise all his companions. It is pure hypocrisy to hate them all or the overwhelming majority of them.

**3. Qadarites:** They rejected the divine determination and decree and were comprised of two groups. The first group appeared in the time of the Companions and claimed that Allāh does not have prior knowledge of events, which is disbelief. The second claimed that man is an independent creator of his own deeds outside the domain of Allāh's creative power. The errors in these views have been discussed earlier. Though this group died out, their ideas were inherited by others, such as the Muʿtazilites and Shīʿites.

**4. Murji'ites:** They claimed faith is restricted to the heart's belief alone, or to the heart's belief and tongue's affirmation alone and that deeds are not from the reality of faith and that faith does not increase or decrease. Hence, they expelled deeds from faith and asserted that they were not essential for salvation. This is similar to what Paul (Saul of Tarsus) did with respect to the teachings of Jesus (عَلَيْهِ السَّلَامُ). He abolished the necessity of the law in salvation, thereby disfiguring the religion of Jesus, which was Islām, *inward submission* with *outward compliance*. The Murjiʾites were of varying levels in their error and misguidance: Those who say faith is knowledge (maʿrifah) alone; those who say faith is the heart's assent (taṣdīq) alone; those who say it is only the expression of faith on the tongue alone; and those who say it is the heart's belief coupled with the tongue's affirmation alone. They all divorced works from faith.

**5. Jahmites:** They employed Greek philosophical concepts—acquired through argumentation with Hellenized Jews, Sabeans and Christians—to formulate a new, innovated theology regarding Allāh's

---

[64] The Bāṭiniyyah (esoteric) groups include the Qarāmiṭah, ʿUbaydiyyah, Qāzilbāsh, Khurramiyah, Ḥashshāshīn and others. They brought together a mixture of Persian, Magian beliefs, Greek philosophy and the external face of Shīʿism as a means of misguiding Muslims.

*essence, names, attributes* and *actions*. It led them to reject the names, attributes and actions of Allāh through philosophical speculations. The approach of this group in this field were inherited by other sects such as the **Muʿtazilites**, **Ashʿarites** and **Māturīdites**. They also exaggerated in the divine decree and claimed man has no free will at all and is compelled in his actions. They also claimed that faith is *mere knowledge* of Allāh's existence in the heart and nothing more. This doctrine is an invalidation of Islām from its very foundations, since it treats everyone who inwardly acknowledges a creator [such as Jews, Christians, Hindus, Satan, Pharoah and others] to be Muslims. This sect is not considered to be within Islām.

**6. Muʿtazilites:** This group inherited and championed the Qadarite belief that man creates his own actions independently and the belief of the Jahmites in negating Allāh's names, attributes and actions. They put reason over revelation, and claimed that when the two clash, reason is given preference. They created turmoil at the end of the second century of Islām through inquisitions, instigating the rulers to slaughter thousands of Muslim scholars who rejected their heretical doctrines. They are represented by the Modernists of today who undermine the Qurʾān and Prophetic traditions through the application of short-sighted, subjective reason.

**7. Ṣūfīs:** The starting point of Ṣūfism appears to the naive and unwary as an innocent form of spirituality and purifying the soul. However, its end point is a philosophical, mystical system comprising the doctrine that nothing exists except Allāh, that all of existence is but Allāh—an idea called *the unity of existence* (waḥdat al-wujūd) and hence, everything and anything worshipped *is* Allāh. Therefore, *all religion is valid* and innumerable paths to Allāh exist. This is the doctrine of *the unity of religions* (waḥdat al-adyān). As a result, the invocation and worship of saints finds easy justification. Most who enter this path are unaware of its true reality, seeing only the spiritual side, and may never fathom the reality of the system due to the way it is clothed with dubious terms having double meanings.

These innovated doctrines have been successively transmitted throughout the ages until today. Umbrella groups such as the **Muslim Brotherhood** (al-Ikhwān al-Muslimūn) and its offshoots resemble the Khārijites in their doctrines and activities. From them Ḥizb al-Taḥrīr, al-Qaedah and ISIS. The **Conveyance Party** (Jamāʿat al-Tabligh) is an umbrella group for promoting versions and strands of Sūfism. Many **modernist, liberalist** and **rationalist** individuals and groups operate on the principles of the Muʿtazilites. The **Ashʿarites** and **Māturidites**, two similar groups that have a large presence today, have inherited doctrines from the Jahmites, Murjiʾītes and Ṣūfīs. The **Hezbollah** are hardcore Shīʿites.

As for the spoilage inherent in **innovations in worship**, to avoid this, a person must stick to the Prophetic way (Sunnah). All acts must agree with the Sunnah in: *number* (ʿadad); *timing* (zamān) where applicable; *location* (makān) where applicable; *specific manner of performance* (kayfiyyah); the *underlying cause* of the act of worship (sabab); and *type* (jins). A greater understanding of this subject ought to be pursued as it is outside the scope of this work.[65]

In summary, to avoid spoilage of one's water (faith) one must seek the way of the **Righteous Predecessors** (al-salaf al-ṣāliḥ) who are the Companions of the Prophet (ﷺ), their students and their students. They learned, enacted and transmitted the way of the Prophet. The route to that is through the upright, righteous scholars who follow this way in every generation. Equally as important—alongside seeking the truth and acting upon it—is that a Muslim must know and shun all falsehood and avoid the innovations and heresies which are widespread. The Prophet (ﷺ) said: "*I have left you upon clarity, its night is like its day [in distinctness]. No one deviates from it except that he is destroyed.*"[66]

**Sackage.** This refers to looting, pillaging and dismissing. When a person is sacked from a job, the job becomes vacant, empty. In our parable it refers to the attempts to ransack you and make you lose your water (faith) altogether, leaving your vessel completely empty, with nothing left, not even a drop.

Factions of people exist of varying backgrounds who desire that you disbelieve or return to disbelief if you previously left it for Islām.

---

[65] The concise book "*Innovation in Light of the Perfection of the Sharīʿah*" by Shaykh Muḥammad bin Ṣāliḥ al-Uthaymīn is available online and in print.

[66] Refer to *al-Silsilah al-Ṣaḥīḥah* of al-Albānī, (2/648), no. 937.

They have ideological and material motives which are often coupled with hatred and jealousy. If they cannot sack your Īman, they will try to force as big a compromise as possible.

Here are the main factions;

**1. Hypocrites:** They exist in all times, proclaiming belief while concealing disbelief. They can never be known for sure, since Allāh alone knows what is in the hearts of people, therefore we cannot pass judgement upon individuals. They are countered with knowledge, by exposing their lies and schemes and affirming the truth through the tongue and pen. These hypocrites appear in many forms, shapes and guises: as reformers, modernists, rights activists and so on. Desiring sackage, they wear the cloak of Islām so that their views appear as legitimate internal dissent and hence, more easily acceptable. They desire to undermine Islām, reduce it to irrelevance and thereby make people disbelieve just as they themselves disbelieve internally.

**2. Apostates:** There are many Shiʿītes, Qadianis (Aḥmadīs)[67] and people of various backgrounds who never understood Islām to begin with or were practising some unorthodox, deviant form of Islām. On seeing the falsehood and repugnance of their doctored version of Islām and whatever injustice and opposition to reason it comprises, they abandon Islām while having many grievances and harbouring many grudges. Thereafter, they try to convince others to abandon Islām by spreading lies and misunderstandings. Sometimes, people accept Islām hypocritically (see the Qurʾān, 3:72), then disbelieve shortly thereafter in order to put doubts into the hearts of others.

**3. Atheists:** They give divine qualities to nature using highly technical and cryptic language as a means of escaping the gratitude they ought to give for the innumerable favours they enjoy on a daily basis, all on account of pride and arrogance. They resent that there should be an authority over the universe and look for theoretical justifications for this resentment. They believe in conjectures regarding the origin of the universe and life and try to convince others of their positively asserted religious belief that life is purely accidental and matter has intelligent self-organising capabilities.

---

[67] They are non-Muslims to begin with, they believe that Mirza Ghulām Aḥmad (d. 1908) was a prophet, though he was an exposed imposter.

When trying to blame Islām (or religion in general) for *poisoning everything* and being *the source of evil*, they forget that the biggest mass murderers in history were materialists, atheists and that their philosophies such as Darwinism "undeniably comforted racists, sanctioned imperialism and actively promoted eugenics."[68]

**4. Radical Feminists:** There are numerous spiteful, hateful women from Irān (Shīʿism), Africa, the Middle East, India and other Asian nations who have had extremely bad experiences in their personal lives wherein local cultural practices, unjust parental behaviours or family circumstances limited, exploited or harmed them. Being scarred emotionally, they harbour grudges and grievances. This leads them to highly provocative, anti-Islām activity usually in Western lands. They appear as rights-activists and are promoted by private interests and media corporations for their usefulness in shaping and forwarding agendas. They are equipped with selective facts, lies and statistics. They want Muslim women to pour out all of their water (faith) and if not, then as much of it as possible. They presume that intelligent Muslim women who freely choose to protect their chastity and modesty are oppressed, just like they were. They wish to deny Muslim women the freedom to exercise their choice and free will without coercion, all in the name of feminism and human rights.

**5. Religious Interests:** Evangelical, fundamentalist Christians have large-scale strategic operations in place in order to draw Muslims away from the pure and sincere worship of the Lord of Abraham, Moses, Jesus (عَلَيْهِمُ السَّلَامُ) and Muḥammad (صَلَّى اللَّهُ عَلَيْهِ وَسَلَّمَ), to the worship of triads, trinities, saviours, spirits and crosses based on a mythical Jesus manufactured with Hellenic, Roman and Pagan mystery religion concepts. They use a sophisticated system of polemics in their missionary activities based upon their ideologically motivated and extremely biased study of Islām, the Qurʾān and the Prophet (صَلَّى اللَّهُ عَلَيْهِ وَسَلَّمَ). They use the presence of extremist, terrorist groups such as al-Qaeda, ISIS and Boko Haram to argue Islām is a false religion, conveniently forgetting their extremely violent past in which they raped, pillaged and wiped out the indigenous populations of America,

---

[68] Depew, D.J. & Weber, B.H. *The Fate of Darwinism: Evolution after the Modern Synthesis*. Biological Theory 6 :89. (2011).

Africa, Asia and Australia, slaughtering hundreds of millions in the name of Jesus and the Glory of God. They are well-funded, active and collaborate with hypocrites, apostates and radical feminists.

**6. Corporate Interests:** Muslim inhabited lands in Africa, Asia and the Middle East have drawn tremendous political and corporate interest over past decades because of their strategic locations, extreme resource-richness and very large, economically exploitable, growing young populations. Corporate interests may not be anti-Islām in principle but nevertheless, they work to undermine Islāmic beliefs, morals and values, purely for financial interests.

**7. Political Interests:** They are of various backgrounds and desire to usurp Muslim inhabited lands for historical, political, religious and racial reasons and as such, have their share of anti-Islām propaganda. These political interests are powerful, wealthy, have long reach and actively support some of the groups mentioned above. They support vilification of Islām and its adherents through media outlets in order to restrict opposition to the geopolitical activities they sponsor and support in which men, women and children are dispossessed of their lands and homes and often tortured and killed in the process.

**In summary:** A useful, actionable parable has been given through which a person can prevent spillage, spoilage and sackage of his or her Islām, Īmān and Iḥsān—*the three levels of sound religion.* **Spillage** arises when a person is not in control of his soul and its whims. **Spoilage** occurs when a person's faith loses its odour, colour and taste due to impurities. This diminishes the effect faith has, just like water, changed in odour, taste and colour alters its effectiveness. **Sackage** is when hostile elements work to strip a person of his faith altogether, and if not, then to sabotage it as much as possible.

A person is commanded to strive in the worship of his Lord until certainty comes to him:

وَاعْبُدْ رَبَّكَ حَتَّىٰ يَأْتِيَكَ الْيَقِينُ

"**And worship your Lord until there comes to you the certainty (death).**" (15:99).

A Muslim should always proceed upon firm, sound knowledge, and always display patience, forbearance, kindness and justice in the course of maintaining his Islām and Īmān.

## Closing Notes

Finally, the reader should know and understand that mankind was once united upon Islām. Allāh (عَزَّوَجَلَّ) said:

كَانَ النَّاسُ أُمَّةً وَاحِدَةً فَبَعَثَ اللَّهُ النَّبِيِّينَ مُبَشِّرِينَ وَمُنذِرِينَ وَأَنزَلَ مَعَهُمُ الْكِتَابَ بِالْحَقِّ لِيَحْكُمَ بَيْنَ النَّاسِ فِيمَا اخْتَلَفُوا فِيهِ

**"Mankind was [of] one religion [before their deviation], then Allāh sent the prophets as bringers of good tidings and warners and sent down with them the Scripture in truth to judge between the people concerning that in which they differed.**" (2:213).

Islām was the message of Noah, Abraham, Moses, all the Prophets of the Children of Israel (Jacob) including Solomon, David and also that of Jesus, John and finally, Muḥammad (صَلَّىٰٱللَّهُعَلَيۡهِوَسَلَّمَ).

Allāh (عَزَّوَجَلَّ) said:

شَرَعَ لَكُم مِّنَ الدِّينِ مَا وَصَّىٰ بِهِ نُوحًا وَالَّذِي أَوْحَيْنَا إِلَيْكَ وَمَا وَصَّيْنَا بِهِ إِبْرَاهِيمَ وَمُوسَىٰ وَعِيسَىٰ

**"He has ordained for you of religion what He enjoined upon Noah and that which We have revealed to you, [O Muḥammad], and what We enjoined upon Abraham and Moses and Jesus.**" (42:13).

It is the very nature of Tawḥīd (monotheism) and Islām to unite mankind regardless of race, culture, status, class or language.

Allāh (عَزَّوَجَلَّ) said:

وَمَا أَرْسَلْنَا مِن رَّسُولٍ إِلَّا بِلِسَانِ قَوْمِهِ لِيُبَيِّنَ لَهُمْ

**"And We did not send any messenger except with the language of his people to explain clearly to them.**" (14:3).

Every messenger expressed the same meanings comprised in the words salām (peace), Islām (submission), muslim (submitter) and tawḥīd (monotheism) in his respective language.

From this perspective, the Prophets are considered brothers with an identical message. The Companion, Abū Hurayrah (رَضِيَٱللَّهُعَنْهُ) reported that the Prophet (صَلَّىٰٱللَّهُعَلَيۡهِوَسَلَّمَ) said, "*Both in this world and in the Hereafter, I am the nearest of all the people to Jesus, the son of Mary. The prophets are paternal brothers, their mothers are different, but their religion is one.*"[69]

[69] Related by Imām al-Bukhārī in his compilation of Prophetic traditions.

Whoever grasps the above will perceive the capacity of this simple, powerful and compelling message to unite mankind—as they once were—upon a simple, innate, intuitive universal truth.[70]

Other than the name of Islām, the names of all religions are contrived and invented and do not reflect the true, original message of pure monotheism (tawḥīd) and submission (Islām) which every Prophet came with. In their doctrinal formulations, they are in violation of the order, regularity, balance, truth and justice upon which the universe stands and persists. Deviation from this message facilitates the exploitation of man by man and his subjugation in various fields of human activity. This is why Islām is liberating, not subjugating. It is also why tremendous propaganda is waged against Islām by ideologically and materially motivated special interest groups who lose out when people choose to follow it.

In true religion there is only one deity to whom worship and devotion is exclusively directed. There is no racism, class distinction or caste system. There is no superior gene or race. There is no sainthood, priesthood or clergy assuming divine office or holding monopoly over salvation. The connection to the Creator is personal, direct and requires no gatekeepers or intermediaries.

Any way of life that is based upon class discrimination, tribalism or is exclusive to a race or ethnicity is known automatically not to have come from Allāh (عَزَّوَجَلَّ). If all humans are accountable and responsible then the message should be attainable for every person regardless of race, colour, class and circumstance. The message of Islām is clear, simple and intuitive, and innate human disposition is naturally inclined towards it.

All praise is due Allāh and may peace and blessings be upon the last and final Prophet, Muḥammad, his family and companions.

---

[70] At the same time, Islām acknowledges cultural diversity and the variant habits and customs of people so long as they do not comprise falsehood, oppression, harm or moral corruption.

# Bibliography

1. ʿAbd al-ʿAzīz b. Bāz. *Al-ʿAqīdah al-Ṣaḥīḥah wa Mā Yuḍādduhā*. (1420H).
2. ʿAbd al-Qādir b. Muḥammad ʿAṭāʾ al-Ṣūfī. *Al-Mufīd Fī Muhimmāt al-Tawḥīd*. Dār Aḍwā al-Salaf (1428H).
3. ʿAbd al-Raḥmān b. Muḥammad bin Qāsim. *Majmūʿ Fatāwā Ibn Taymiyyah*. (1425H).
4. Dāwūd Burbank. *The Most Beautiful Names Belong to Allāh*. Lecture series (2002).
5. Ibn al-Qayyim. *Madārij al-Sālikīn*. Dār al-Kitāb al-ʿArabī (1414H).
6. Ibn al-Qayyim. *Al-Fawāʾīd*. Dār al-Yaqīn (1418H).
7. Muḥammad Āmān al-Jāmī. *Sharḥ al-Uṣūl al-Thalāthah wa Mukammilātihā*. Dār Ibn Rajab (1435H).
8. Nādir b. Saʿīd al-Taʿmurī. *Huṣūl al-Maʾmūl bi Tartīb Ṭarīq al-Wuṣūl ilal-ʿIlm al-Maʾmūl lil-ʿAllāmah al-Shaykh al-Saʿdī*. Dār Ibn Ḥazm (1424H).
9. Ṣāliḥ al-Fawzān. *Silsilah Sharḥ al-Rasāʾil*. Dār al-Maʾthūr (1436H).
10. Ṣāliḥ Āl al-Shaykh. *Sharḥ al-Ṭaḥāwiyyah*. Dār al-Āthār (1429H).
11. Ṣāliḥ Āl al-Shaykh. *Sharḥ Faḍl al-Islām*. Dār al-Ḥijāz (1429H).
12. Saʿūd b. ʿAbd al-ʿAzīz al-ʿArīfī. *Al-Adillah al-ʿAqliyyah wal-Naqliyyah ʿalā Uṣūl al-Iʿtiqād*. Takwīn (1436H).